Testing Spoken Language

CAMBRIDGE HANDBOOKS FOR LANGUAGE TEACHERS

General Editor: Michael Swan

This is a series of practical guides for teachers of English and other languages. Illustrative examples are usually drawn from the field of English as a foreign or second language, but the ideas and techniques described can equally well be used in the teaching of any language.

In this series:

Testing
Spoken Language

A handbook of
oral testing techniques

Nic Underhill

CAMBRIDGE
UNIVERSITY PRESS

Published by the Press Syndicate of the University of Cambridge
The Pitt Building, Trumpington Street, Cambridge CB2 1RP
40 West 20th Street, New York, NY 10011–4211, USA
10 Stamford Road, Oakleigh, Melbourne 3166, Australia

© Cambridge University Press 1987

First published 1987
Seventh printing 1993

Printed in Great Britain at the University Press, Cambridge

Library of Congress cataloguing in publication data
Underhill, Nic.
Testing spoken language.

(Cambridge handbooks for language teachers)
Bibliography
Includes index.

1. Language and languages – Ability testing.
2. Language and languages – Examinations. 3. Oral
communication – Ability testing. 4. Oral communication –
Examinations.   I. Title   II. Series.
P53.6.U5 1987   001.54′2′076   86–31052

British Library cataloguing in publication data
Underhill, Nic.

Testing spoken language: a handbook of
oral testing techniques. – (Cambridge
handbooks for language teachers)
1. Language and languages – Study and
teaching – Great Britain. 2. Language and
languages – Ability testing
I. Title
418′.0076   P57.G7

ISBN 0 521 32131 X hardback
ISBN 0 521 31276 0 paperback

WD

Contents

Contents

Acknowledgements

My thanks are due to Clive Jaques, John de Jong, Mike Levy, Keith Morrow, Don Porter, Bill Shephard, Norman Whitney, Protase E. Woodford and my colleagues at International Language Centres, for their ideas, encouragement and help; and to Ush for her invaluable common sense.

Introduction

This introduction is divided into six sections:

Section 1 describes who the book is intended for;
Section 2 presents a model;
Section 3 asks why such a book is necessary at all;
Section 4 summarises the themes on which the book is based;
Section 5 is a glossary that defines some testing terminology for the
   purposes of this book;
Section 6 explains the order and content of the chapters.

WHO IS THIS BOOK FOR?

This handbook is intended for teachers and other people who are
interested in the use of oral tests of language ability; an oral test being
defined as a test in which a person is encouraged to speak, and is then
assessed on the basis of that speech. The book is aimed at any kind of
language teaching programme where it is desired to produce an oral test
that will fit in with the teaching programme and that will be designed by,
or in full consultation with, the teaching staff themselves. The sequence of
this book follows the order in which a new test programme would
logically be carried out; starting with preliminary questions about needs
and resources, then presenting different oral test types and tasks to choose
from, and finally discussing the marking system and evaluation of the test
in practice.

Answers to questions in chapter 1 will affect choices in chapter 2, which
will in turn constrain the choice of testing and marking techniques in
chapters 3 and 4. Although they are presented in this logical sequence,
these different steps in the test programme are not distinct operations to
be carried out one at a time, independently of each other. To produce the
'best' test, you will need to consider how decisions made in one area will
affect your freedom of choice in another.

The book does not assume any knowledge of language testing as a
specialist discipline and is written for practising language teachers. It
deplores the cult of the language testing expert. All the examples of test
types are in English, but they could equally well be applied to oral tests in
other languages.

1

A MODEL

The model below is sometimes used to identify the different components involved in communication by speech. The arrows indicate the direction of speech. They point in both directions; at one moment, one person is listening to the other person speaking, and the next moment, the roles may be reversed. The speaker becomes the listener, and the listener becomes the speaker. These switches from one role to another often happen very fast in conversation. Speech is normally a two-way system of communication: situations where only one person speaks and others only listen, such as an academic lecture or a political address, are comparatively rare. This feature of interactive role-switching distinguishes good oral tests from other language tests; listening, reading or writing tests which present a set of questions and elicit a set of answers are clearly not interactive in this way.

With one addition, the same model can be used to represent the oral test situation. As well as a person who speaks and a person who listens, in an oral test we need somebody to assess that speech. It is this process of assessment that turns it into a test.

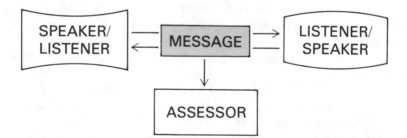

In an oral test, you do not need to have three different people, one for each role. Chapter 2 uses variations of this model to describe and compare different test types. Some types of oral test have more than three people, some have fewer: self-assessment, for example (see 2.1) needs only one person. The most common type of oral interview involves two people, the learner and a person who is both listener and assessor. (See below.)

This test type, for example, is economical but it does require somebody to carry out two roles at the same time, and this can be difficult to do.

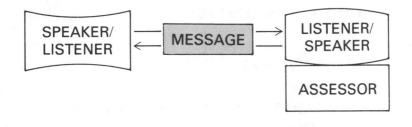

WHY A BOOK SPECIFICALLY ON ORAL TESTING?

Oral tests are qualitatively different from other kinds of tests. They do not easily fit the conventional assumptions about people and testing, which are examined below. There is a lot of interest now in oral testing, partly because teaching is more than ever directed towards the speaking and listening skills, particularly in the early stages. Naturally, this should be reflected in the testing. In order to free oral tests from the burden of conventional language testing wisdom, they should be considered as a class of their own, and that is the purpose of this book.

Why have oral tests generally received little attention? Many books have been written about language testing. They follow the changing fashions of language teaching, but they usually make the same basic assumptions about the nature of language testing. Generally, little space is devoted to oral testing compared to testing the other skills. This is partly because of the difficulty of treating oral tests in the same way as other more conventional tests.

The most striking assumption in these books is that it is the test itself that is important, while the human beings who take the test, and those who mark it, seem less important. Tests are seen as objects with an identity and a purpose of their own – you can see many references in the literature to the 'test instrument' – while the learners are often remote figures who are only of interest for their reactions to this instrument (the usual term in testing research for test-takers is 'subjects'!). The number of possible ways they can react is strictly limited. Similarly, the preference for easily marked, multiple-choice or limited-response tests reduces markers to the role of machines. Because of this, learners do not *enjoy* taking tests, and teachers do not enjoy marking them.

In a genuine oral test, this order of priorities is reversed. Real people meet face to face, and talk to each other. The 'test' may not even exist, in the same way that a written test does, on paper. It is the people and what passes between them that are important, and the test instrument is secondary. In fact, with a technique like an oral interview, it becomes impossible to talk about the 'test' independently of the people involved in it because it doesn't have a separate existence as a set of questions on paper.

It follows that oral tests must be designed around the people who are going to be involved. This is a human approach; we want to encourage people to talk to each other as naturally as possible. The people, not the test instrument, are our first concern.

Where do these conventional assumptions about testing come from?

The most important influence on the development of language testing has been the heritage of psychometrics, in particular intelligence testing. 'Psychometry' is the measurement of the human mind, and in the first half of this century a lot of time and effort was devoted to proving that there was a single measurable attribute called general intelligence – the 'g' factor – which we all possessed in different quantities. The 'g' factor was said to be related to parental and racial hereditary traits and to social background. Virtually all the statistical techniques used in language testing today were developed to a high degree of sophistication fifty years ago or more in the drive to prove this biological basis of intelligence. These techniques in current use in testing include correlation, regression and the analysis of variance, as well as item analysis, item discrimination, and various test reliability formulae.

The fact that the statistics actually proved nothing at all did not lead to the assumptions being challenged; it merely meant that ever more complex statistics were developed that *would* prove the initial assumptions of the researcher. These 'sophisticated statistics poised on testing techniques of rustic simplicity' (see Appendix II) became incomprehensible to the layman, and encouraged by the experts, led to an even stronger belief in the invincibility of statistical methods. This invincibility is so strong that it can easily withstand cases of scientific fraud, such as Cyril Burt's deliberate falsification of his data on twins in the 1950s.

This sounds like a remote chapter of history, interesting but irrelevant to the subject of language testing. However, it is relevant, because the same assumptions of mechanical measurability and statistical invincibility exert a strong influence on our attitudes today. In the late 1970s, the field of language testing research was revolutionised by the use of a sophisticated new technique called factor analysis, which takes the scores obtained by the same people on a number of different tests and extracts a number of different *factors*, which are supposed to relate to fundamental mental abilities.

In particular, factor analysis was supposed to prove the existence of a single factor of general language competence, which is related to performance on different language tests to a greater or lesser extent. (This, too, was affectionately known as the 'g' factor.) The implication was that all tests, including oral tests, were only partial reflections of this basic underlying language competence. Fashions change, however, and now, only a few years later, the Unitary Competence Hypothesis, as it was called, has been largely forgotten.

Was factor analysis a 'new' technique? Not at all; it was invented in the first years of this century, and was used in exactly the same way to support the argument that there was an underlying general intelligence trait and that different tests merely reflected this more or less strongly. The issue was neither proved nor disproved convincingly; it rumbles on to this day. The Unitary Competence Hypothesis has suffered the same fate. The point is not that statistics are always wrong; as sets of figures, they are inherently neutral. But they must be treated with caution; it is easy to believe that they prove or support a theory when in fact they don't.

Psychometrics wanted to be a science. Those aspects of human behaviour that could be predicted and measured were emphasised; those aspects that were unpredictable or inconsistent were ignored. The test techniques developed then, particularly the multiple-choice format so familiar to us now, offered the learner no opportunity to behave as an individual. The statistics developed then and used today interpret human behaviour as basically similar, and conceal any form of self-expression. Such behaviour was described as 'variance', and a lot of effort was put into reducing the amount of variance a test produces.

Language teaching inherited this belief that language proficiency, like general intelligence, was a single, underlying mental factor, and that therefore the measurement of language by a test was essentially the same process as the measurement of length by a tape-measure or temperature by a thermometer. The assumption carried over from intelligence testing was that the language proficiency of an individual is at a single point on a linear scale, and that this point can be determined by an objective test instrument. All you have to do is develop the right instrument.

Language testing has developed enormously in recent years and has absorbed many other influences of a more pragmatic nature. We no longer believe that there is a single scale of language proficiency. Anyone with any experience of oral testing in particular will know that oral ability cannot be forced into such a mould. But the criteria we use for evaluating tests still favour the statistical assumptions of the mental testing heritage, and the result is a strong bias towards mechanical tests and against the human face of oral tests.

This book is an attempt to redress that imbalance. It recognises that oral tests, because they involve a subjective judgement by one person of another, are likely to be less reliable; but it suggests that the human aspect of that judgement is precisely what makes them valuable and desirable. When we test a person's ability to perform in a foreign language, we want to know how well they can communicate with other people, not with an artificially-constructed object called a language test. If we are willing to question the assumption that statistics must come first, we can then start from the idea of the best possible test for a particular context and work to strike the right balance between the human and the statistical forces.

SUMMARY OF THEMES

1. *You need full local knowledge.* Tests are not inherently good or bad, valid or invalid; they become so when they are applied to a particular situation. You cannot say how good a hand-tool is unless you know exactly what it is used for; similarly, you can only evaluate a test in a specific context.
2. *You need to design the test as a whole.* Following on from a full awareness of the local conditions, an oral test must be conceived as an integral whole, and usually as a natural complement to the teaching programme. It's no good asking one person to draw up the aims, another to decide on the test techniques, and a third to design the marking system. The entire procedure should appear as a single and consistent entity to testers and learners alike.
3. *You need a human approach.* Oral tests must treat people as human beings. In small ways, as well as in the design of the test procedure in general, we can make taking a test challenging, instructive and even an enjoyable experience. There is a good practical reason for this, not just that it is nice to be nice; if you treat people in as friendly and human a way as possible they will tend to respond in kind, and you are going to get a much more accurate picture of their oral ability.
4. *You need to find a suitable balance.* The planning and execution of an oral test involves making positive compromises between different forces, for example, between communicative and structural aims, between impression and analytic marking systems, and between highly reliable and highly valid techniques.
5. *You need to adapt and improve.* At the same time, the balance is dynamic – no test procedure is sacred. Test evaluation is not something you do once, then sit back and relax; it is a continuous process. The best test reflects any changes in the aims of the programme or the needs of the learners. There are so many factors that have to be considered in the design of a test procedure that it would be surprising if circumstances did not change from time to time.

GLOSSARY

The words described below are often used in testing, but with different meanings by different writers. This glossary is not intended to provide universal definitions that will work in every context; it gives working definitions of testing terms used frequently in this book, in order to help the reader understand the author's meaning.

Oral test An oral test is a repeatable procedure in which a learner speaks, and is assessed on the basis of what he says. It can be used alone or combined with tests of other skills.

Learner A learner is a person who takes a test in a foreign language. This is preferred to *student*, as a person taking a test may not be a student at the time; we are all learners, whether or not we are students. It is also a better label than *testee* or *subject*, both of which are unattractive and have connotations of the laboratory animal under experimental observation.

Interviewer An interviewer is a person who talks to a learner in an oral test and controls to a greater or lesser extent the direction and topic of the conversation. While exercising this control, she may nonetheless yield the initiative to the learner to redirect the discussion to another area. An interviewer also takes the role of the assessor, or one of the assessors. As there are so many possible variations in the roles of interviewer, interlocutor and assessor, interviewer is used as a cover-all term in this book for the person who conducts the test and deals directly with the learner.

Interlocutor Some oral tests have a person whose job is to help the learner to speak, but who is not required to assess him. An interlocutor is a person who talks with a learner in an oral test, and whose specific aim is to encourage the learner to display, to the assessor, his oral fluency in the best way possible. An interlocutor is not an assessor. She may well be known to the learner, for example, as a teacher.

Assessor An assessor is a person who listens to a learner speaking in an oral test and makes an evaluative judgement on what she hears. The assessor will be aided by pre-defined guidelines such as rating scales (see 4.7), which give considerable help in making these judgements. Ultimately, the decision is a subjective one, which is to say that it is a human one made on the basis of judgement, intuition and experience. Having more than one assessor usually means a more reliable judgement (see 4.1).

Marker This term is reserved for someone who is not present at the test itself but later awards marks to the learner on the basis of an audio or video tape recording. This may be a routine part of the marking system (see 4.3, second marking) or it may be an occasional exercise for the purposes of *moderation*. This definition of marker reflects its use for people who correct other types of language tests; they mark the papers but they never meet the individuals who wrote them. Assessors do meet the individuals; this is one reason why assessing is different from marking and why oral tests differ from other tests.

Rater The term is used in this book as a synonym for marker. An *examiner* is a person who marks or assesses performance in standardised and large-scale language test batteries, usually containing tests of several different kinds. While an oral test may well be included in such batteries, such examinations are outside the scope of this book.

Communicative   When a learner says something that is relevant and true (for himself at least), to someone else who is interested and has not heard it before (from that speaker, at least), then that act of speech is communicative.

Any definition of this term will be incomplete, and invite correction, or at least addition. For example, no mention is made here of the continuous interactive exchange between speakers which is characteristic of normal conversation. This is a minimal working definition. This book describes techniques and procedures as more communicative or less communicative rather than the black-and-white terms communicative or non-communicative. The term is used in this book in a neutral sense – a more communicative test is not necessarily a better one. A number of less communicative techniques are included in the following chapters; there are many circumstances in which it is desirable to use these as well as, or instead of, more communicative techniques.

Authentic   An authentic task is one which resembles very closely something which we actually do in everyday life. To engage in free conversation is an authentic task; to transform sentences from active into passive or present to past is not authentic. Note that this is not the same thing as communicative. Copying out a shopping-list or an address is authentic but not communicative; and there are many communicative exercises, for example of the 'information gap' kind, which are not authentic.

Objective   An objective test is one in which there is a single correct answer, or a very small number of possible correct answers, for each question. The marker only has to decide whether a learner has given the right answer to each question, and she is not required to exercise any personal judgement. In theory, an objective test could be marked by a machine; sometimes they are.

This is the central meaning of *objective*; the opposite is *subjective*, and both are neutral terms for particular types of tests; they do not have any positive or negative connotations. Some situations would call for one type, some for the other type. Perhaps both can be used.

Unfortunately, they have also acquired connotative values which suggest that a subjective test is necessarily bad and an objective test is always good. This will tend to be true if you are very concerned with statistical reliability (see 5.4); but if you are very concerned with communicative validity, then the reverse is true. Objective tests are easier to mark but they are almost always less realistic.

Stimulus   A stimulus is something that is intended to encourage the learner to speak, usually by providing a subject to talk about. It might be a picture, a text, an object or a particular topic. Its use in this book does not have any of the technical meaning of the automatic stimulus/response theory of behaviourist psychology.

Validity   As a general term, does the test measure what it's supposed to? Having specified the aims of a test at the outset, the purpose of validation is to find out if in fact it meets those aims. Different forms of validity are discussed in more detail in chapter 5.

Reliability   Does the test give consistent results? If the same learners are tested on two or three occasions, do they get the same score each time?

Evaluate   To evaluate a test is to find out how well it is working, in the widest sense. Is it valid? Is it reliable? Does it take too long? Are the learners and the assessors happy with it? Does it meet the specifications?

Moderate   Moderate has a more restricted meaning, concerning test reliability. To moderate a test is specifically to compare the way different assessors award marks, and to take steps to reduce any discrepancies.

Best test   This is the test most suitable for the particular situation in which it will be used. Although every test procedure has its own advantages and disadvantages, it is only a good test or a bad test in a particular context. If somebody asked you what the best car is, you would probably say that it depends on what you want to use it for; a Jeep is better than a Jaguar for driving over rough ground, and a Mini is better than a Cadillac for driving round a small, crowded town. Because the best test is context-specific, it can only be designed for, and produced in, that context, and no amount of expert authority will make the best test in one place automatically the best test in another.

He and *she* are used throughout the book as referring to the learner and the tester/interviewer/assessor respectively. By this means, the presence and involvement of people of both sexes may be implied, while the potential ambiguities of pronominal reference are avoided.

At the end of the book are two appendices. Appendix I describes three oral tests that form part of publicly available test batteries, to show how some of the testing and marking techniques described in this book are used in practice.

Appendix II contains a number of bibliographical references and suggestions for further reading. In the interests of readability, and to further the aim of demystifying testing by removing the shadow of the expert, the main text contains no references at all.

Introduction

THE STRUCTURE OF THE BOOK

The order of the chapters follows the steps in the development of an oral test procedure.

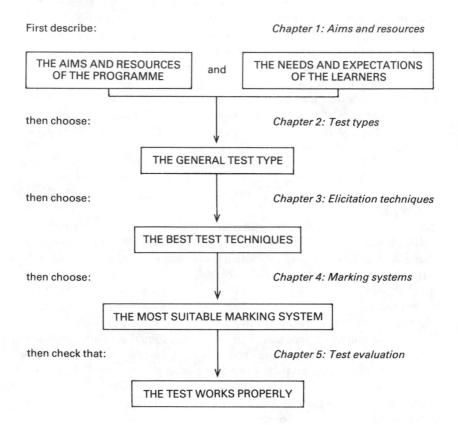

First describe: *Chapter 1: Aims and resources*

| THE AIMS AND RESOURCES OF THE PROGRAMME | and | THE NEEDS AND EXPECTATIONS OF THE LEARNERS |

then choose: *Chapter 2: Test types*

THE GENERAL TEST TYPE

then choose: *Chapter 3: Elicitation techniques*

THE BEST TEST TECHNIQUES

then choose: *Chapter 4: Marking systems*

THE MOST SUITABLE MARKING SYSTEM

then check that: *Chapter 5: Test evaluation*

THE TEST WORKS PROPERLY

1 Aims and resources

This chapter asks a number of questions about the general background in which the oral test is to be designed and used. Sections 1 and 2 ask about the institutional aims and resources, and sections 3 and 4 ask about individual needs and expectations. There are many different types of oral test and marking systems, and the answers to the questions posed in this chapter will make it easier to select the most suitable techniques from the following chapters.

The first section asks the question we should ask before we start any new project: why exactly are we doing it? If you know precisely what the aims of the project are before you begin, it will be much easier to take the right decisions later on. When you reach the evaluation stage (see chapter 5) it will also be easier to decide if you have achieved those aims. The question is not always as easy to answer as it sounds; many language tests are given because it is the accepted practice to give language tests as part of a teaching programme, without setting out clear aims.

A written multiple-choice test is usually held in scheduled lesson time in an ordinary classroom, without the need for any special arrangements. Oral tests, on the other hand, can often be more difficult to design, administer and mark. It is all the more important, therefore, to make sure that you know in detail the purpose of the test before you begin and so prevent resources being wasted on producing a test that is unsuitable.

Available resources are the subject of the second section. When you know what the aims are, the next question is: what resources do we have to help us achieve those aims? These resources include people, time, space and equipment. Every oral test technique requires slightly different resources, and the best test will consist of techniques which match the resources available. For example, choosing a test that requires a brief interview with a native-speaker if you have lots of time but only one native-speaker available, would be an inefficient use of resources.

The third and fourth sections ask about the needs and expectations of the learner. The person who takes a test is the immediate consumer of the product; when manufacturers are designing a new chocolate bar or style of furniture they go to great lengths to find out what their potential customers need or want. In the history of language testing, on the other hand, we have often managed to ignore the point of view of the test-takers altogether. A good oral test allows learners to be treated, and to behave, like ordinary human beings, so it seems right that we should do a market survey of what they think, expect and want.

1.1 Aims

Why have a test at all? Giving a test is like asking a question – it is a request for information. If you ask the right sort of question, you get the right sort of answer. If you ask a silly question, you get a silly answer. In order to develop a test, you have to know what kind of information you want.

Tests can be used to ask four basic kinds of question. (A fifth kind of test, asking about an individual's innate aptitude for language learning, does not usually include oral techniques.)

1.1.1 Proficiency: what is the learner's general level of language ability?

A proficiency test aims to produce a single score result: usually it quickly covers a wide range of language in order to find a broad target level, then zeroes in on that level for fine-tuning. A live oral test can be an economical way of testing proficiency because the interviewer can very quickly decide what the broad target level is, and then concentrate on the fine-tuning. Unlike a written or recorded test, where a lot of time can be spent answering and then marking questions which are either much too easy or much too difficult, most of the oral test period is spent on language tasks pitched at more or less the right level.

To get a complete picture of a learner's language proficiency, you would need to use a test battery, consisting of several tests of different kinds – structure, extended writing, and listening tests, as well as an oral test. However, a well-designed oral test which incorporates a number of different test techniques will give a quick and quite accurate measure of general proficiency. If desired, written or comprehension tasks can easily be built into such a test.

1.1.2 Placement: where does this learner fit in our teaching programme?

The information being sought here is an accurate placement. A placement test identifies the right class for a particular learner; there is no such thing as a good score or a bad score, only a recommendation for the most suitable class. Obviously, the interviewer must know which classes or levels are available; her task then is to decide in which of the pigeon-holes – the range of available classes, or none of them – to put the learner. 'Pigeonholing' is a useful way to look at placement testing; the fewer the options available, the more consistent the decisions will be.

The interviewer should also know a lot about what happens in those classes. Ideally, she should be a regular class teacher herself so she knows the classes well and can ask herself questions like, 'How would I feel if this learner appeared in my class tomorrow?'

To assist her, precisely-worded rating scales (see 4.7) will be very useful. These rating scales should be closely related both to the performance objectives for the course (what do we want the learner to do at the end of the course that he couldn't do at the beginning?) and to the basis of the course syllabus. If syllabuses are based around sequences of grammatical structures, for example, then a placement test should place learners according to their knowledge of these structures.

1.1.3 Diagnosis: what are the learner's particular strengths and weaknesses?

A diagnostic test offers the learner the opportunity to use a range of language elements – they might be functions, structures, situations or vocabulary – to find out which he is familiar with and which he is not. It does not produce information in the form of a score, but as a list of areas in which the learner is strong and those in which he needs further practice or remedial work. The interactive nature of an oral test allows the interviewer to probe for individual strengths and weaknesses, to ask for repetition or clarification, perhaps to elicit the learner's own opinion of his ability, and still leave the learner feeling good at the end of the test.

1.1.4 Achievement: how much has the learner learnt from a particular course?

An achievement test takes a sample of the language elements or skills that have been covered on the course and aims to test how well the learner has mastered those elements. The result is normally expressed in terms of an overall score, although there is also a diagnostic element; the course teacher will want to know which of the course contents were successfully learnt and which weren't. This knowledge will help her with future course planning. The best result is when every learner gets an excellent score.

In reality, most test programmes will combine two or more of the above aims. For example, a placement test may also aim to diagnose any very weak areas and an achievement test will often aim to test general proficiency as well as how much students have learnt from a particular course. It is very important to design a test programme that meets all of its aims, and most oral test techniques can be adapted to a variety of purposes. In an oral test, the marking system is as important as the test itself in meeting the aims of the programme.

GLOBAL VS ANALYTIC TESTS

The general assumption made throughout this book is that the techniques described are being used to test overall oral proficiency. This is not always the case: an oral test may be intended only to test a specific feature of spoken language, either:

a) because the only purpose of the test may be to test that feature,
or
b) because the test is designed as a series of techniques, each one concentrating on one or two particular features, and the results are put together to form a cumulative overall rating.

Where the techniques described in this book are particularly suitable for testing a particular feature – such as structural accuracy, or the use of connecting words – this is usually pointed out in the descriptions. However, this has not been done on a rigorous basis, by saying which specific components of oral proficiency each test is good for, and therefore by implication which it isn't, because the aim is to encourage experimentation and adaptation, and not to limit the reader to the conventional wisdom.

In practice, oral tests frequently consist of several different testing techniques which are marked using different criteria. For example, marks might be awarded, in the first part, for structural accuracy and correctness of pronunciation; in the second part for breadth and appropriateness of vocabulary, and in the third part for fluency and communicative effectiveness. In each case, the techniques and the marking systems obviously need to be carefully designed to match.

A single test technique, marked on an overall oral proficiency criterion, will give a quick but approximate estimate of speaking ability. A sequence of different techniques, each marked on the basis of one or two different sub-skills of speaking, with their scores added together, will clearly take longer but should produce a more accurate and consistent result. As always, the choice of test design depends on the aims and resources of the programme.

The advantages of sequencing different test techniques together are examined in more detail in chapter 2, section 2.10; and the use of different categories for marking in chapter 4, section 4.5. The use of different categories for self-assessment is described in chapter 2, section 2.1.

1.2 Resources

A testing programme can only be successful if it is designed to be carried out using the available resources. There are three different kinds of resources: people, time and physical facilities.

1.2.1 People

In testing, as in teaching, people are the biggest asset, and like any other resource, they can be used effectively or badly. Most obviously, you need enough people to administer as many tests as will be needed without difficulty. Depending on the marking techniques used, you may also need people to mark or re-mark the tests afterwards. You will also need people to develop and try out the test in the first place, and subsequently to check that the testing programme is effective, and to improve it if necessary. You will certainly need people to carry out administrative duties, particularly getting learners to the right place at the right time, and making sure they are prepared and know what to expect; then to present the results as quickly as possible in the desired form, while also keeping a record for subsequent reference.

In a large testing programme, all these different tasks will be done by different people with different qualifications and skills. In the most simple case they will all be done by the same person, who tests people whenever necessary, completes an assessment, tells the learner about it and records the result. Neither a big programme nor a small one is inherently better; the important point is to design a test system that uses the people available in the most effective way to meet the aims of the programme.

Ask yourself how many people in each of the following categories will be available to help with the testing programme.

a) People with oral testing and marking experience.
   A lack of experienced testers would suggest using more controlled techniques where learner responses to each question will be more predictable; these can be anticipated and discussed during the training programme.
b) Teaching staff and administrative staff.
   As far as possible, use people for tasks which match their existing abilities. Training should be given for any unfamiliar tasks requiring more than basic common sense. This is as true for interviewing as it is for marking.
c) Native and non-native speakers.
   A lack of native speakers means that test techniques should not

require raters to make on-the-spot judgements about subtle distinctions of language use. Where a programme is dealing with learners from a monolingual background, native speakers of the target language are not necessarily preferable. Native speakers of the learner's mother tongue will be more sensitive to the learner's background and circumstances, and better able to put the learner at ease. A combination of one mother-tongue speaker and one target language native speaker can make a successful and balanced team, each picking up on points the other misses.

1.2.2 Time

First of all, the test development stage: how much time do you have to develop the test? Test development always takes longer than you think. Sharing the work only saves time when mechanical tasks, such as checking answer keys or proof-reading, are involved; otherwise, more people means more time. However, it should also mean a more balanced test. Is it needed as soon as possible, or do you have time to follow the kind of sequence described in chapter 4, section 4.2?

Secondly, the test operation stage: how much time will the staff be able to devote regularly to carrying out the testing procedure? Is a lack of availability likely to restrict the times at which the test can be offered? Given the number of testers at your disposal, the amount of time they have to spend on testing, and the number of tests they will have to conduct, what is the maximum amount of time that can be spent on each test?

Just as learners' performances drop if a test goes on too long, so the consistency of interviewers' ratings falls quickly when they get tired. It is better to use fewer or shorter techniques than risk having interviewers who are frequently tired or under pressure; it is impossible in these circumstances to maintain an objective and positive frame of mind, and this attitude conveys itself very quickly to learners.

Finally, the test improvement stage: once the test is in operation will you be able to make adjustments to the techniques and marking systems, or does the whole test procedure have to be as perfect as possible before it is introduced?

Will you be able to set aside a couple of hours a week for someone to monitor the test continuously? Or, if the test is to be taken on certain specific dates only, will you be able to do a thorough follow-up check after each session? If not, how do you propose to make sure the test works?

Will you want statistical validation of the test procedure (see 5.4–5.6)? Do you already have the expertise to carry this out?

1.2.3 Equipment and facilities

Which of the following physical resources are available to be used for testing?

a) rooms and furniture for testing and preparation
b) sound or video recording equipment
c) photocopying, printing or duplication facilities

Some careful thought in advance about the choice of room and the arrangement of furniture can make a big difference to the atmosphere in which the test is conducted. Tests should be held somewhere that is quiet and free from interruption. Anybody trying to hold a conversation will become irritated if repeatedly disturbed by noise or by other people; a learner taking a test will also get the feeling that his test has not been given a very high priority. He may also lose his train of thought or flow of speech, and so lose confidence.

At the same time, a test that is to be a regular part of a teaching programme should be held in familiar surroundings, such as an ordinary classroom. The furniture to be used can be rearranged away from the blackboard or teacher's desk, to reduce the feeling of a teacher questioning a student. For a test involving one learner at a time, two or three chairs and an ordinary table can be set up in a neutral corner of the room, carefully placed with regard to heat, fresh air, light and so on.

The chairs of the interviewer and the student do not have to face each other on opposite sides of the table: they can be arranged at an angle or even side by side. This is particularly appropriate if they will be looking at pictures or texts together and there is no reason why they cannot look at the same picture. If a third person is present to assess or observe, but not actually to take part, she should sit a bit further away, so that she is not physically in the area where the conversation is taking place.

Where the test involves several learners (see for examples 3.2, 3.3, 3.6) they can sit in a circle in the centre of the room, or round a table if a professional atmosphere is desired. If the interviewer is to take an active part in the discussion she will obviously join the circle; otherwise, she should sit outside or withdraw as soon as she has set the discussion going.

If the oral test programme is to run continuously, rather than once a month or once every three months, a separate room can be used specifically for this purpose. It can then be set up with comfortable furniture, in an informal arrangement in attractive surroundings, to make the test-taking experience as pleasant as possible. The danger is that the testing room or booth will become a torture chamber for learners, and a test that should be regarded as a routine occurrence becomes a special event that can only be held behind closed doors in a special room (see also 2.11).

Equipment to be used for recording oral tests (see 2.8) should be easy to operate, give good quality reproduction and, above all, be reliable. It does not have to be the best or most expensive. Top quality and top price equipment requires more experience to use and will need more careful attention and maintenance. Extra equipment may be needed to give better sound or picture quality, and the operator will need more training. All this makes the recording process more intrusive and distracting, as well as more expensive. Unless really high-quality recordings are required, it is better to use ordinary classroom equipment – so long as it has been proved reliable in operation!

1.3 Needs

The *aims* discussed in section 1.1 were *institutional* aims: they answered the question, 'What is the purpose of having a testing programme at all?'

Needs are *personal*; they are not necessarily the same as aims. This section asks the question, 'What does the individual learner stand to gain – or lose – from taking the test?'

In ideal circumstances, the aims of the programme match the needs of the learner so that the teaching/testing programme provides just what the learner most needs, and everybody is happy. In the real world, however, there is often a mismatch between institutional aims and personal needs, resulting in a test which is of little or no benefit to the learner, and may have a demotivating effect. Such a mismatch may stem from a large and inflexible training programme, particularly in an industrial setting; or it may result from a learner's greater awareness of his own special needs, and hence a greater sensitivity to whether those needs are being met.

Different people have different needs – at a personal level and at a professional level. If there are a few clearly distinct groups – classified, for example, by present occupation or future training course – you can prepare and use certain techniques or stimuli accordingly.

If there is a wide variety of different individual needs, the overall aims of the programme may be to teach and test general English, because there are not sufficient resources to develop materials for each special area. However, an experienced teacher will always adapt her lessons as far as possible to suit the individual needs of her students; and an oral test can be flexible in the same way. Unless there is a testing programme which demands that each learner is given exactly the same test, the interviewer can adapt the test by choosing the techniques or topics of discussion to suit individual needs. If she does not already know what these individual needs are, she can quickly find out at the beginning of the test by asking, 'What is your job?' or 'Why are you learning English?'

Making the test relevant to the learner's needs is not just an academic exercise. If the learner realises that the interviewer is sufficiently interested in his personal needs to adapt the test accordingly, he will respond to that expression of interest. He will probably have more to say about topics that concern him personally. He will not necessarily perform better, but he will feel that the test is more relevant for him, and the assessment will be based on a more representative sample of his language.

Needs usually become evident in the course of a short conversation with the learner. This discussion can, in fact, form part of the test (see 3.1, 3.5, 3.7). If more detail is required, the tester can consult some of the recent literature devoted to this subject (see Appendix II). The development of needs analysis models took place at roughly the same time as the development of the communicative approach, and in some cases the term 'communicative' was used to mean 'relevant to the individual learner's particular needs'. This is a specialised, even esoteric, use of the word, and it is not the sense in which it is generally used either in this book or elsewhere.

There is a paradox in the use of needs analysis models for analysing personal language needs. They are sophisticated and it requires a degree of sensitivity and experience to use them effectively. The paradox is that when they work well, you generally don't need them, and when you do need them, they don't help much. They work well in cases where a learner clearly needs certain types of language which can be confidently described; the favourite examples of this kind being waiters and airline hostesses. In most cases, however, the learner's needs are more elusive, and it becomes difficult to predict with any confidence exactly what he will and will not need to say.

Needs analysis models can be useful checklists to make sure you have asked the right questions and not missed anything important out. Beyond this, they make common-sense questions into a complicated and often irrelevant process.

1.4 Expectations

How learners react to a test, and therefore how well they do, depends on how the test compares with what they expected it to be like. These expectations can make nonsense of a carefully prepared test. If they are not used to the type of test, what are their reactions likely to be? Would it be a good idea to give them some preparation for the test in advance? Should the test procedure be explained in the mother tongue? Will learners expect to be able to discuss the test with each other? Does this matter?

Every culture values education highly but does so in different ways. A test should be designed to match the local educational philosophy, as far as this is consistent with the aims of the programme. A test procedure designed for use in a culture which values logical analysis will get different reactions in a culture which gives more weight to rote learning; but if the test is part of a programme that aims to teach analytical skills, then the test must clearly reflect this too.

There may, therefore, be a discrepancy between the *objectives* of a teaching/testing programme and the *cultural expectations* of the learners. As oral tests allow the personal side of the learner to come through more than in written tests, they will be particularly sensitive to this discrepancy, and can produce distorted and inaccurate results. In such a case, the test will reflect the degree of familiarity with the culture with which the objectives are associated rather than just oral proficiency.

If this discrepancy concerns only the type of tasks to be performed in the test, this can easily be remedied by explaining exactly what is expected of the learner, and giving him the opportunity to practise, if necessary. An instruction sheet can be prepared in the mother tongue and distributed to learners in time for them to ask questions if desired.

The problem will be greater if the learners lack the particular skills or strategies necessary for the test tasks. For example, a skill such as summarising or picking out the key points (used in such techniques as in 3.2, 3.12, 3.13) or a strategy such as making inductive generalisations from specific examples (often used in discussion of a picture or text) may take a considerable time to acquire. Unless the test is deliberately intended to discriminate between learners on the basis of their possession of such skills and strategies, the tasks should be chosen to avoid them. (Such a deliberate intention might be for diagnostic or aptitude testing.)

To help compile a profile of the learner's expectations, here is a list of points to check. It is important to bear in mind that the process of using such a checklist should bring out, rather than conceal, the differences between individual learners. An average learner profile will not actually represent anybody at all and may be quite misleading.

- What is the learner's educational background?
- How strongly is it influenced by his cultural background?
- What kinds of language tests has he previously taken?
- Are his expectations of the teaching/testing programme essentially academic or vocational?
- How old is he?
- What is his general level of proficiency?

In short, is there a discrepancy between the learner's expectations and the aims of the programme? How serious is it? What can be done to remedy it?

Anticipating the likely level of learners may be difficult, but it can have an important influence on the design of the test. Certain question types and techniques are particularly suitable for certain levels, and to produce the best test you therefore need to know the most likely range of levels. An Oral report (see 3.2) or a Role-play (see 3.4) will be too difficult for beginners or elementary learners; a straightforward Question and answer (see 3.9) exchange is usually quite easy, and will not discriminate between good and very good speakers. Similarly, the development of Rating scales (see 4.7) and Mark categories (see 4.5) will depend on the likely levels of proficiency.

2 Test types

This chapter discusses some general types of oral tests in preparation for the detailed descriptions of elicitation techniques described in chapter 3. It invites the reader to select the broad test characteristics that most suit her answers to the questions in chapter 1; and having done that to go on to choose the most suitable elicitation techniques described in greater detail in chapter 3. Where appropriate, the general test types outlined in this chapter are cross-referenced to the detailed test techniques in chapter 3.

2.1 Self-assessment

This is the easiest, cheapest and quickest form of assessment. It can be done by post, over the telephone or as a spoken or written question. It can stand alone or form a small part of a larger oral test (for example, see techniques 3.1, 3.5, 3.7).

When we are talking to other people, whether in our mother tongue or in a foreign language, we are constantly assessing how successful our communication is. We do this by listening to ourselves as we speak, by watching what effect it has on other people's appearance and behaviour, and by what they say in reply. This self-assessment is usually unconscious because in genuine communication we do not have time to monitor ourselves consciously; but we do notice when communication breaks down, or somebody reacts in a totally unexpected way: 'He just didn't seem to understand!' or 'What did I say wrong?'. Over a period of time, we get a general impression of how well we can communicate in a foreign language, and it is this general impression that we want to elicit in a self-assessment.

In this sense, the learner is in the best position to say how good he is at speaking; he has been present at every effort he has ever made to communicate in the foreign language, while oral test assessments are usually based on a sample of ten minutes' speech!

All learners have the ability to determine their own oral proficiency within certain limits. What they lack is the experience that enables the professional teacher or tester to compare that learner against an external standard. The test must therefore provide easily understood guidelines that will enable each learner to express in an explicit form his intuitions about his own level.

This is another way of saying that we should be teaching the learner to know how he is getting on independently of the teacher. We ought to be doing this anyway, as an automatic part of our teaching, to enable learners to take more responsibility for helping themselves progress. Any teaching programme that pays more than lip-service to the idea of student-centred learning should be training learners to monitor and assess themselves.

Self-assessment is unlikely to be an adequate measure of oral ability on its own because of a variety of different factors that affect people's judgements of themselves. These may be conscious and deliberate factors, such as over-rating to try to impress or get a better job; or under-rating to stay in a comfortable and unchallenging language class. Unconscious factors include the differing degrees of self-confidence and perceptiveness that learners bring to the task of self-judgement. A history of unspectacular and unenjoyable academic achievement will probably lead the learner to underestimate his abilities. Women in general will often rate themselves lower than men when they are, in fact, at least as good; similarly, older learners will often rate themselves lower than younger learners.

Such factors are connected with personality and socialisation, and are subject to a great deal of variation; they are not measurable and predictable, and the tester or test user must therefore become as sensitive as possible to sources of bias among the learners she is dealing with. The more homogenous learners are – in terms of age, sex, nationality, and educational background, for example – the more they will give comparable judgements. This does not mean that their self-assessments will necessarily be more accurate: just that they will tend to share the same bias!

Self-assessment can be introspective, where the learner is asked to reflect back on his foreign language experience and rate himself against some kind of scale; or it can be based on a specific speech sample elicited by any of the techniques described in chapter 3. In the latter case, the self-assessment – in the form of a simple question after the test – can be used instead of, or as well as, any other marking technique.

Some techniques will be easier to self-correct than others. Sentence transformation (see 3.19) or sentence repetition (see 3.20) are carried out and self-corrected every time conventional language laboratory drills are used. In fact, self-rating and correction are essential skills if such drills are to be used properly and they can be used to heighten the learner's awareness of his own language. If desired, the tapes can be corrected by the learner himself, and then kept for checking by conventional rating systems. Another possibility is to offer the learner several chances to record his task on tape – whether it is a laboratory drill, a short presentation, or a text read aloud – until he is happy with it, at which point he passes it over to the conventional rater.

Where several learners are involved in a test task at the same time (see for example techniques 3.2, 3.3, 3.4 and 3.6) they can be asked to assess each other as well as themselves. This group assessment requires a lot of mutual confidence and belief in the value of the system, but it makes the judgement more authentic – as in real life, it is the people you are speaking to who decide if you have effectively communicated or not. Comparison between his self-assessment and other people's assessments of himself, using the same scale, will help the learner to make his own self-judgement more critical and accurate.

For introspective self-assessment we can make two distinctions to demonstrate the different kinds of scales used: *defined* versus *non-defined* and *general* versus *specific*. A *non-defined* scale has descriptions only at the top and bottom ends of the scale, whereas a *defined* scale has descriptions for every level in between. A *specific* scale asks the learner to rate his performance in a particular language situation, while a *general* scale refers to the use of language in general terms only.

These two contrasts are presented here as clear-cut and distinct categories; in practice they are not, and often merge into each other. For the present purpose of description, they combine to give four different types of self-rating scale.

The scales, and the instructions on how to use them, are presented in the native language where the learners are from the same language background. A great deal of care over choice of words and examples has to be put into the construction of a self-assessment scale, and it will benefit nobody if learners fail to use it properly because they misunderstand fine distinctions in the foreign language. Self-assessment exercises are not intended to be tests in comprehension. To make the personal comparison as immediate as possible, the scales are often expressed in the first person ('I can . . . ').

TYPE 1: NON-DEFINED GENERAL SCALES

These invite the learner to rate himself on a scale from

        0 – I speak no English at all.

  to

       20 – I am completely fluent.

There are no intermediate-level descriptions and no specific examples to focus on. Separate scales may sometimes be provided for different categories.

TYPE 2: NON-DEFINED SPECIFIC SCALES

Again, these have no intermediate-level descriptions, but invite the learner to consider his likely language performance in a particular hypothetical situation. For example, 'Imagine that you need to ask for a pair of shoes to be changed in the shop you bought them from. How well would you cope?' Answer from

> 0 − I could not cope at all.

to

> 10 − I would have no difficulty.

TYPE 3: DEFINED GENERAL SCALES

These scales have explicit descriptions at every level, but they are expressed in terms of general language abilities rather than specific examples:

- I can only talk about a very small number of topics.
- I can hold an ordinary social conversation with some difficulty, but I am occasionally lost for words.
- I can hold a social conversation on common topics, but I still find it difficult talking to more than one person.

It is desirable to express scales like this example in the most positive terms possible ('I can . . . ') but to make fine distinctions accurately, positive and negative statements usually need to be taken together ('I can . . . but I can't . . . '). These scales are similar in form to the kinds of rating scales used by test assessors (see 4.7). As with different categories in assessors' rating scales, self-assessment scales are quite likely to ask for several assessments in different areas, and can take the form of multiple-choice questions, such as:

Fluency and naturalness: When you speak in English, do you . . .
a) always construct the whole sentence in your head first?
b) frequently have to think about what you're going to say?
c) sometimes have to pause to think of the right words to use?
d) speak with only occasional hesitation?

Vocabulary: How many words do you think you know and use in English?
a) less than 250
b) 251–750
c) 751–2000
d) 2001–5000
e) 5000+

Connecting sentences: How easy is it for you to speak several sentences together in a connected way?
a) impossible
b) very hard
c) difficult

d) not too hard
e) easy

Error-correction: Do you identify and correct your own errors . . .
a) very rarely?
b) not often?
c) sometimes?
d) usually?
e) always?

As with all scales expressed in such general terms, it is often difficult to decide exactly what the words mean, and where to draw the line between one level and another. If self-assessment is to be used as a regular part of the programme, it is worth having tuition or class discussion about the use of such scales, and thereby making learners more sensitive to their own strengths and weaknesses. The fact that they are so general means that the learner has to do quite a lot of work before he can honestly register improvement on such scales, so they are not suitable for repeated progress testing, except on long-term programmes.

TYPE 4: DEFINED SPECIFIC SCALES

These often take the form of a checklist questionnaire about specific behavioural objectives. For example:

I can: ask about the weather	yes/no
give simple directions	yes/no
spell my own name aloud	yes/no
invite a person to dinner	yes/no
persuade someone to accept	yes/no
accept/refuse such a request	yes/no

The number of 'yes' answers give an overall score. Where a teaching programme has precisely formulated objectives, they can be used as the basis of the questions to be asked. There can only be a limited number of such specific questions, so a pilot questionnaire would need to be tried out to see which questions produce the most accurate score – as compared with a conventional oral test, for example. Self-rating with this type of scale is easier because the questions are more concrete; rather than worry about a global subjective judgement of his own oral proficiency, the learner has only to ask himself a number of questions involving mental translation: 'Would I be able to say that?'

2.2   Teacher assessment

After the learner himself, the teacher is the person who has had the most experience of the learner's speaking ability in the foreign language. Instead of being based on a ten-minute test, a teacher assessment will be based on fifty or a hundred hours' exposure to the learner's language, in a variety of activities and situations. In classical testing terms it is therefore based on a bigger and better sample of language; in individual human terms, the language has been produced under classroom conditions, which should normally mean that the learner was more relaxed and confident than in an oral test. For many people, the test situation itself creates considerable anxiety which can badly affect their performance. A good interviewer encourages a learner to open up and demonstrate his proficiency with the language, but there is a limit to what even the best tester can do in ten minutes; with much more time at her disposal, a successful teacher comes to know her students as people. It is that 'knowing' that a teacher assessment tries to tap.

Teacher assessment can be carried out either on the spot or as a continuous assessment over a period of time. A third possibility is to base the assessment on a specific period of, for example, one week; during that period the teacher takes care to ensure that every learner has an equal opportunity to speak. In each case, the teacher will use a rating scale (see 2.1, 4.7). For a spot judgement, there might be a specific situation described to help focus the mind:

> If the learner found himself in the foreign country today, and had to make his way from the airport to the town centre, book into a hotel and contact somebody by telephone, how well do you think he would cope?

Or,

> How fully would the learner be able to take part in a detailed discussion about his own professional or academic field of interest?

For a continuous assessment, the teacher's judgement is formed as a gradual process rather than as a sudden decision. Each time the learner attempts a task in class, the teacher has, in effect, administered a single-item test. The total of all these tests administered throughout a course constitutes a complete test of proficiency, and unlike a short oral test, will not be influenced by short-term individual variations such as nervousness, illness or fatigue on a particular day. A carefully kept teacher's record of her learner's daily oral performance will make an excellent cumulative oral test.

The disadvantages of teacher assessment are principally concerned with reliability.

a) The more people involved in an assessment programme, the more difficult it is to be confident that the results are comparable.
b) It may be difficult to arrange thorough training for all the teachers involved. Good teachers do not necessarily make good assessors.
c) When rating their learners, teachers will tend to make assessments by comparing each learner with others in the same class. Even when using an absolute rating scale, teachers tend to apply it relatively. If one class has a generally higher level than another class, the ratings made may not be comparable on an absolute basis.
d) Teachers build up relationships with learners over a period of time. These are generally constructive and have a positive effect on learning, but not all relationships will be the same. Like all human beings, teachers react in different ways to different people, and this may be reflected, if only subconsciously, in their assessments. Similarly, learners react differently to different teachers, and will be more talkative in some classes and less so in others.

These problems are not insuperable, however, and given the benefits of teacher assessment, are well worth tackling with a careful rater-training programme (see 4.2).

2.3　Who does the learner speak to?

If an oral test is defined as one in which the learner has to speak, who is he going to speak to? Apart from tests recorded in a language laboratory (see 2.8 Recording oral tests) there are four possibilities.

– He can speak to an interviewer who is also the assessor.
– He can speak to an interlocutor, who is not involved in assessment.
– He can speak to another learner.
– He can speak to a group of learners.

2.3.1　Learner–interviewer/assessor

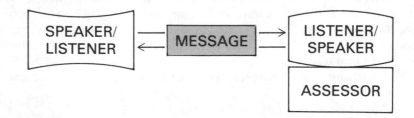

The roles of interlocutor and assessor are combined. This is the most common and most economical, but it is difficult for one person to concentrate on assessing effectively while at the same time trying to appear interested in what the learner is saying and involved in serious communication with him. This dual role is particularly tiring, and frequent rest breaks are necessary.

2.3.2   Learner–interlocutor

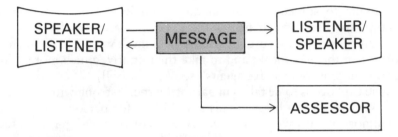

Here, the interlocutor is distinct from the assessor, and is able to give her full attention to managing the discussion and encouraging the learner to speak as fluently as possible. If she is a native speaker or teacher, however, the interlocutor will probably be seen by the learner as being the assessor's assistant, rather than as a completely independent person whose job is to help the learner. When you talk to a native speaker of a foreign language, you are usually aware that your speech is not as fluent or as accurate as hers. Talking to a native-speaker interlocutor may make the learner feel at a disadvantage.

The learner is still on his own, but instead of a single, combined interviewer/assessor, he now has to perform in front of two people. This is more difficult for some learners. The value of having a separate interlocutor depends very much on how successful that individual is at projecting the right image to the learner – independent, friendly, and concerned for the learner's best interests.

2.3.3   Learner–learner

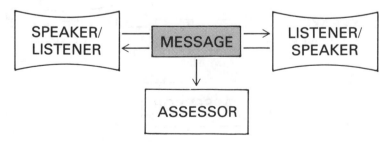

Two learners speak together to carry out a set task, while the assessor listens without intervening. She is able to give her full attention to what they are saying, since she no longer has to worry about keeping the conversation going and eliciting fresh language. This saves considerably on examiner fatigue, and avoids the interviewer appearing tired and disinterested to learners because she has asked the same questions many times before that morning, while they are doing it for the first time.

Rather than talking to a native speaker or teacher model, which inevitably puts their own best performance in the shade, the learners feel they are talking to someone of about their own level whose interests are identical to theirs which makes the communication as fluent and as successful as possible. It usually makes them more willing to speak, to say more when they do speak, and to take the initiative much more. 'There were no victims, only active agents' (see Appendix II).

Some care needs to be taken in pairing learners, strong with strong and weak with weak, both for linguistic level and for personality. Learners will almost always work together rather than compete, but in cases of extreme mis-matching, the assessor may decide that one learner has not had a fair opportunity to speak, and ask for him to do the test again with a different partner.

2.3.4 Learner–group

A group of three to six learners carry out a set task together. The assessor remains silent throughout, and preferably should not be involved even in setting the situation up and briefing the learners. As with 2.3.3 above, learners tend to be less inhibited and more spontaneous in their speech because they are working with a peer group of other learners. Interacting

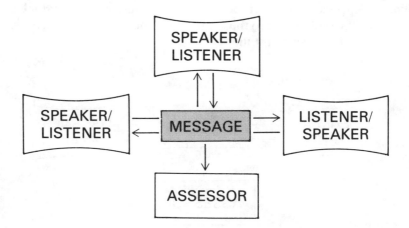

with more than one other person is highly authentic and generates a spontaneity and group creativity which is lacking in most oral tests.

For the assessor, keeping track of five or six different people is clearly harder than evaluating two, but the interaction can be allowed to run on much longer – say twenty to thirty minutes – giving plenty of time to each in turn, while still being quicker than a series of individual oral tests. Some learners will always be quieter and harder to place than others; the assessor should quickly assign rough ratings to the more prominent personalities, and concentrate on every utterance of the less talkative members of the group.

Where learners are talking in pairs and groups, their performances can be judged by the assessor not only on what she personally thinks of what they have said, but also on the visible reactions of the other learners. In some circumstances, members of the group can even be asked to rate each other, using the kind of rating scales described in 2.1; but unless there is a strong sense of mutual trust among the group this may only serve to weaken the feeling of co-operation.

There are many possible techniques described in the next chapter which can be used or adapted for pairs or groups of learners, for example:
3.2   Oral report
3.3   Learner–learner joint discussion/decision making
3.4   Role-play
3.6   Learner–learner description and re-creation
3.11 Using a picture or picture story
3.15 Reading aloud

2.4   The direct interview type

Techniques of this type, discussed in chapter 3, are:
3.1 Discussion/conversation
3.5 Interview
3.7 Form-filling
3.9 Question and answer

The direct interview is the most common and most authentic type of oral test for normal purposes; there is no script and no preparation on the learner's part for any special activity. Obviously, the interviewer will be well prepared, but not so rigidly as to control exactly what the learner says. This flexibility means that there will be a considerable divergence between what different learners say, which makes such a test more difficult to assess with consistency and reliability. As well as an assessor training programme to allow for this, there should be adequate opportunity to discuss and practise the skills of interviewing so the interviewer can get the best out of the learner in the shortest possible time.

This type of test is therefore expensive in terms of the selection and training of interviewers and assessors. Where the resources exist, however, it is the most satisfactory way of starting an oral test, as the inherent flexibility allows other test techniques to be chosen or adapted as the interviewer thinks suitable. For example, it is often thought to be difficult to discriminate between higher levels of proficiency using a direct interview test alone, whereas it can lead into other techniques which discriminate better.

2.5   The pre-arranged information gap

Techniques of this type, discussed in chapter 3, are:
3.6   Learner–learner description and re-creation
3.11 Picture story, variation 1

An information gap between two learners, or between a learner and the interviewer, is deliberately created by the test designer. The learner's success and speed in bridging that gap is taken as an indication of his oral proficiency. This type of test is effective at producing clear evidence of communicative success or failure; but it is restricted to a specific type of communication – the transfer of factual information. Factual information is very important, and we certainly do communicate a lot of it, but the world would be a very boring place if that was all we ever spoke about.

At the design stage of information-gap tests, there is a danger of creating a task that is too much like a problem-solving test. In other words, the ability to reason analytically may be as important to success as the ability to speak fluently. The quick thinker will do better than justified by his level of English, and the divergent or non-linear thinker will get caught out by logic rather than language.

Role-plays (see 3.4) are similar in that the learner is an actor in a pre-arranged drama rather than a free agent speaking for himself. The test designer constructs the situation and so lays down the broad outline of what will be said; the learner is left to fill in the gaps with his own words. This can be a comforting support for the learner who is terrified of having nothing to say; or it can seem like an uncomfortable strait-jacket to the learner who likes and wants to share his own views and experiences with others.

2.6 Tests where the learner prepares in advance

Techniques of this type, discussed in chapter 3, are:
3.2   Oral report
3.10 Reading blank dialogue
3.14 Re-telling a story
    The learner has sufficient time before the test to prepare for the task and therefore brings to the test a good idea of what he will say. The time needed for preparation will range from a few minutes for a blank dialogue to several hours or days for a presentation. A prepared oral test gives all the learners something to say without putting words into their mouths; it tests the ability to compose and present statements with care and deliberation rather than the spontaneous self-expression of an interview-type test.

2.7 Mechanical/entirely predictable tests

Techniques of this type, discussed in chapter 3, are:
3.15 Reading aloud
3.19 Sentence transformation
3.20 Sentence repetition
    Other techniques which may be entirely mechanical, or which can leave some room for individual expression, are:
3.16 Translating/interpreting
3.17 Sentence completion
3.18 Sentence correction
Mechanical-type tests determine in advance what the learner is expected to say – there is a single correct answer. All the learners therefore take exactly the same test, and their performance can be easily and directly compared. The tests are quick, and the marking requires no great degree of experience or training. If they are to be marked live rather than recorded, one person can usually act as both interviewer and assessor.
    Their complete predictability makes such tests unauthentic and non-communicative. They do not, on their own, give a realistic evaluation of oral fluency, but are used, as one of several sub-tests, to give a rapid standardised measure of the learner's control of grammatical structure and of the mechanical aspects of speech such as pronunciation, stress and intonation patterns that affect meaning, liaison, elision, and so on.
    Such tests need not be boring. If they are included in the test programme for positive reasons, and teachers and testers regard them as an integral and important part of the test, the learner can be encouraged to look on these tasks as games or challenges rather than mindless manipulations. The attitude of the interviewer during the test is crucial.

2.8 Recording oral tests

Any ordinary oral test can be recorded on tape, but in most cases making a recording is not an essential part of the test. The recording is used subsequently for one or more of four purposes:

- as the basis for assessment (see 4.3)
- as data for moderating the consistency of assessment (see 4.2)
- as the basis for self-assessment (see 2.1)
- as teaching material on which to base correction and feedback

Similarly, a video system can be used to make a recording of a test for subsequent playback and analysis. To a learner, a video film of himself speaking in a foreign language is a powerful external demonstration of his communicative ability because his own mannerisms and the reactions of other people can be seen as well as heard. A series of video-recorded oral tests followed by analysis and discussion of the video can provide the basis for a rapid improvement in communicative effectiveness.

This section is, however, more concerned with a particular type of test which has no live interviewer or assessor at all. It is usually held in a language laboratory where several learners at once respond to pre-recorded stimuli heard through headphones. Their spoken responses are recorded on the tapes in each booth and then collected for marking. These are referred to here as 'recorded tests'.

Note that the arrows only go in one direction. The learner is encouraged to speak and his recorded speech is listened to later by a listener/ assessor, but there is no two-way communication between them and no opportunity to switch roles from speaker to listener and back again, as in live conversation.

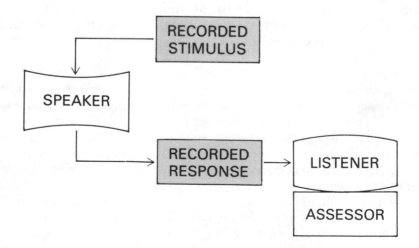

The advantages of recorded tests are:

a) It is possible to test many people at the same time. An average-sized language laboratory has 12–16 booths, so it can be used to give a ten-minute test to more than fifty people an hour, with only a single laboratory operator needed.

b) The test marking does not have to be done in real time, i.e. in the same place and at the same time as the test itself. It can be done where and when convenient, in comfort, with the facility to replay any part of the tape if desired.

c) The marking time for each test can be considerably shorter than the test itself. Most language laboratories have the facility to switch student recorders on and off from the main console while continuously broadcasting a master tape. This enables the operator to turn the machines on to record each learner's response and to turn them off during instructions or longer stimuli. Using this 'test compression', a test lasting fifteen minutes can be marked in only seven or eight.

d) The largely predictable nature of what the learner will say makes it possible to anticipate the most likely responses and produce a detailed marking key (see 4.4). Such tests normally produce reliable marks.

e) Recorded tests can be useful where live interviews are difficult because of practical problems in getting learners and assessors in the same place at the same time; or for personal or cultural reasons, for example young people who are shy or embarrassed to speak openly in front of a stranger.

The disadvantages of recorded tests are:

a) This type of test is not very authentic. There are few situations in the real world in which what the learner says has absolutely no effect on what he hears next.

b) The assessor of a recorded test can *hear* everything a live assessor can, but she can't *see* the test; she therefore misses all the visual aspects of communication such as gesture and facial expression. Even silence often has a visible meaning.

c) A live test in which an assessor can participate can be lengthened or directed if the assessor finds it difficult to evaluate, or has not heard or understood something; but there is nothing a recorded tape marker can do if the learner's speech sample is unclear or unsatisfactory.

d) Technical difficulties can lead to poor quality recordings, or even no recording at all. Recorded tests should be carefully checked at the end of each recording session to ensure, at the very least, that each learner's voice has registered.

e) A recorded test gives the learner nothing to take away – there is no possibility of knowing the score, finding out which class you will be in, or learning anything useful from your errors. There is no human contact in the foreign language.

f) Some people are afraid of speaking into a microphone. They may be unused to a disembodied voice heard over unfamiliar headphones, and therefore so nervous that they fail completely to comprehend the instructions. The recorded-test designer should anticipate such problems by giving instructions in the native language, or in written form, or by ensuring that all learners are familiar with the system in advance; and the operator should monitor all the learners while the test is in progress to make sure that they are all speaking.

2.9 Using the telephone

Some learners now require a foreign language only for use over the telephone, and most learners will need to speak the foreign language on the phone sooner or later. More and more, we use the telephone for getting information, passing messages or making arrangements that we would previously have done in writing. Speaking a foreign language on the telephone calls for special skills because:

a) Whereas phone calls in our native language often consist of a social chat with a friend, phone calls in a foreign language are almost always professionally or personally important, with high information content, and little verbal redundancy. It can be embarrassing to ask for repetition, especially more than once!

b) At the same time, the telephone adds a lot of noise interference and distorts certain acoustic aspects of speech in characteristic ways – sibilant and fricative sounds such as /s/ and /f/ are easily confused, and voiced and voiceless consonants can be harder to distinguish. The notorious confusion between thirteen and thirty, fourteen and forty, and so on, is compounded by distortion in the telephone itself.

c) Most importantly, the telephone does not allow us to use the visual component of normal face-to-face communication. We therefore miss all kinds of information from a speaker's face and gestures; we cannot tell visually when he is about to speak, when he has finished speaking, or when he wants us to wait while he searches for a word. The exact meaning of certain stress and intonation patterns may escape us if we cannot see the speaker.

Where learners will clearly be needing to use the foreign language on the telephone, an oral test can be easily devised that is wholly or partly conducted over the phone. Many of the test techniques described in chapter 3 can be adapted for testing on the telephone. Particularly suitable are:
3.4   Role-play, variation 2

3.5   Interview
3.6   Learner–learner description and re-creation
3.7   Form-filling
3.13 Variation 2, Passing the message on

Some techniques are actually made more communicative and realistic by the fact that the speaker and hearer cannot see each other. For example, an interviewer who says to a learner, 'What can you see in this picture?' is obviously engaged in an unrealistic language-testing exercise. But it is easy to conceive of a situation in which one person is asking another over the telephone to describe a picture which the first person cannot see.

A whole oral test can be conducted by phone over any distance. In circumstances where learner and interviewer would not normally be in the same place at the same time, the low cost of a ten-minute phone call provides an economical alternative. If a learner is travelling from a distant country to follow a short, intensive language course, and nothing at all is known about his level, the price of a brief placement phone call will be more than compensated for by the advance notice about the learner's language level, needs and interests that it will give the teaching staff.

At the other extreme, a telephone test can be carried out on an internal phone system, with the learner either originating the call or responding to it. The other person may be another learner in another room, an interlocutor, or any other suitable person who is available. If no such internal system exists, a cheap intercom will do. The assessor may be on the other end of the phone line from the learner; or she may be in the same room with him, listening to his phone conversation with someone else (an interlocutor or other learner, for example).

Where the telephone is used as one technique in a face-to-face oral test, the learner can be instructed to answer the phone when it rings. He then has to deal with one or more incoming calls, for example:

– to reply to a wrong number call
– to take a simple message
– to take a garbled or incomplete message and ask for elaboration
– to provide simple information, e.g. from an internal directory.

2.10   Sequencing test techniques

The oral test techniques given in chapter 3 may seem to be a number of individual tests to be used quite independently of each other. This impression is misleading because it is rare for an oral test to consist of just one technique. Usually it consists of several techniques placed in a sequence which may either be fixed in advance or left to the interviewer's discretion and experience.

Why have more than one technique in a single test?

a) It is more *authentic* to use a mix of techniques, with the learner doing different things with the language – perhaps talking to different people. Unless the learner needs to use the language in one specific way only, a good test will reflect different types of language use. An oral test of language for academic use, for example, might naturally require a sequence of tasks involving picking out key points from a passage, reconstituting an argument from written notes, and engaging in group debate on a specific issue, with perhaps a short text to be read aloud at some point. All the sub-tests can be related to a single theme which is developed as the test progresses, with later sections referring back in content to earlier ones.

b) Since different people are good at different tasks, a *fair* test is one which will present an overall picture of oral proficiency. An oral test that consists only of Question and Answer, for example, will naturally favour learners who are good at answering questions.

c) A sequence of test tasks allows a more *balanced* test to evolve, which mixes more communicative tasks with more mechanical ones, more subjective ones with ones that are more reliable or easier to mark. To help improve the consistency of assessment, a change of task during a test can be used as an opportunity to swap interviewers and so combine multiple tasks with multiple assessment (see 4.1). This creates a natural information gap which can be exploited by getting the learner to pass on a message from one interviewer to the other.

d) A live test with several different parts is more *flexible* and can be adapted quickly to meet changing circumstances or different needs. One or two techniques can be included for trial purposes, without being included in the score, to see how they can be adapted or improved. If time is suddenly very short, one or two techniques can be omitted or shortened or local current affairs can be spontaneously included in a discussion section to allow the learner the chance to give his natural and unprepared opinion. An experienced interviewer will be ready to vary the contents of a test to suit the level, age and background of each learner, just as we do when we speak to different people in the outside world. Somebody who has difficulty reading, unconnected with his oral ability, should not be asked to read aloud, nor should a person with poor sight be asked to describe a picture.

It is this flexibility of a live oral test that distinguishes it from conventional tests. Language tests are normally prepared entirely in advance, with every question and every word carefully planned (and because of this, they usually have to be kept secret from the learners!). Oral tests can be planned and conducted like this, too; a fixed series of techniques, each with a fixed series of questions, is determined and laid down as the correct test procedure to follow. This produces a standardised test, but one which does not exploit the potential flexibility of live oral tests.

In at least part of an oral test sequence it is highly desirable that there is enough flexibility in the procedure for the interaction to alter the direction. 'Sequence of techniques' may mean 'variety': you don't necessarily have to do the same things always in the same order. At the most basic level, the interviewer varies the questions, and the order of questions, to suit each learner. Similarly, things the learner says and the way he responds to particular tasks may make the interviewer decide to use a different technique. This is an authentic reflection of normal conversation; depending on how a person is behaving, and which way the conversation is going, we may decide to delay saying something, to introduce it a different way, or not to say it at all.

If this flexibility is planned into the test procedure, it is a good idea to have a checklist of points to cover. The interviewer does not have to use particular techniques in a particular way, but in order to make sure that she has not missed anything out, she has a checklist of types of language to elicit at some stage of the test. Here is an example of a checklist:

— Can the learner use polite social formulae?
— Can he spell his name?
— Can he describe his own reasons for learning English?
— Can he ask for repetition politely?
— Can he ask you simple information questions?
— Can he narrate a series of events in the past?
— Can he produce continuous and connected speech?

This checklist does not tell the interviewer exactly what technique to use: there are different ways of eliciting questions. But it does ensure that while the test procedure is flexible, it none the less elicits similar language from each learner, which helps to ensure both reliability and validity (see chapter 5).

2.11   Timing and location of tests

How many parts a test has, and how long each test takes, will be determined by the aims and resources of the programme (see chapter 1). As well as the *duration of the test* itself, time must be allowed for *preparation* and *giving instructions* where necessary. One way to reduce testing time is to use techniques with an *optional cut-off*. Discussion about the *location of the test* should consider the role of the test in the overall programme as well as the physical resources available.

2.11.1   Duration of the test

The length of an oral test can be anything from three to thirty minutes; most often, it is between eight and twelve minutes long. In that time the learner will probably produce more of the foreign language than he does in an hour-long written test, so the importance given to an oral test should not be reduced on account of its brevity. An oral test at a higher level of language will usually last longer than one at a lower level, because the learner will need more time to demonstrate his greater proficiency. The more general the aims of a test the longer it will take, in order to yield a representative sample of language on which to base an assessment of overall proficiency.

The personality and background of the learner also influence the length of the test; a person who is lacking in confidence, or who has a sound, passive knowledge but has not spoken in the foreign language for years, will need time to relax enough to show how well he can perform. Many other people will be found to conform to certain typical learner profiles, and can be assessed quickly. To summarise, the best test lasts as long as it takes the interviewer to form a confident judgement.

2.11.2   Preparation

Preparing for a test is something that can take a few minutes or several weeks. A technique such as Re-telling a story (see 3.14) requires the learner to have five minutes to read the story to himself immediately before the test. At the other extreme, many of the best-known public examinations are preceded by courses of up to a year and are specifically intended to prepare learners for a test of two or three hours!

The advantage of test preparation is that it promotes confidence among learners who are then equally familiar with the test content or procedure. This ensures that those who have taken a similar test before do not have an advantage to start with. On the other hand, the more learners are allowed or encouraged to prepare for a specific test the less their perform-ance will represent their ordinary oral ability in a natural situation. The best test is one that is so authentic and flexible that the only preparation possible is successful learning, and 'teaching to the test' becomes impossible.

2.11.3   Instructions

Clear instructions are crucial, otherwise you will test familiarity with the test procedure and not language ability. One way to help ensure everyone has the same degree of familiarity with the test is to have written instruc-tions for all non-obvious techniques. Suggesting a word to fill in each gap on a printed page is obvious to anyone who has done it before, and incomprehensible to anybody who hasn't!

The learner is given the instructions at the start of each technique and can be asked to read them aloud. This ensures that he reads right to the end, and also gives the interviewer a good idea of whether the learner has understand the instructions or not, and if in doubt allows her to intervene and check before going on. This is obviously not infallible, but it's better than the interviewer giving the instructions once orally, and then saying 'OK, did you understand that?' It takes a brave learner to admit he has not understood the instructions in an oral test. Where low-level learners with a common mother tongue are involved, the instructions should be in their own language.

2.11.4   Optional cut-off

The optional cut-off is a way of shortening the test and saving everybody's time. It can be used in situations where it is not essential that all learners are seen to be taking exactly the same test, and only with techniques where items or tasks can be graded in order of increasing difficulty.

The interviewer starts with the easiest items or tasks, and proceeds up the scale of difficulty until the learner has difficulty coping. When he has clearly failed two or three successive tasks or questions, the interviewer returns to a slightly lower level for another two or three items before ending the test. The purpose of this is to confirm the learner's level of proficiency and to restore his confidence. For high-level learners, the test will go on to much harder items; for low-level learners, it will be over quickly.

This technique can be used with:
3.8   Making appropriate responses
3.9   Question and answer
3.11 Using a picture, variations 4 and 5
3.15 to 3.20.

2.11.5   Location of test

A test is sometimes held in a special test room, which is convenient where there is a large daily testing programme or if special equipment is needed. Otherwise, why bother? It only serves to build the test up into something extra special, and makes the learner more nervous than ever. An oral test doesn't need pen and paper, it doesn't need special furniture, it doesn't really need the profound silence of the examination hall. It's much better to demystify it by using an ordinary classroom, or an office, and lend an air of reality to the process.

Hold the test in the corridor, the reception area or the canteen; if the weather is good, try it in the open air – wherever there is room for two people to sit and talk, like ordinary adults going about their ordinary business. The interviewer as well as the learner will be able to relax a little more in natural surroundings, and they can lower the fearful masks of professional tester and unwilling victim that they normally have to wear. A special test in a special room becomes a world apart for all involved, and nobody benefits from that.

2.12 On being friendly

An oral test is a direct meeting between two or more people, and it can provide results that we can't get from conventional written tests. But because it is live, and the interviewer is dealing with a different person every time, she must take great care to present herself as an interested and friendly person, and not as an interviewer conducting her fifteenth identical test of the day. If you treat your testee like a specimen under a microscope, you can expect to get a thoroughly defensive and suspicious performance. Try to be human, and you will get a more human response.

There are several friendly things that you can do.

2.12.1 Before the test:

- Use the learner's name (first name or family name as appropriate).
- Identify yourself – put a name to the faceless tester!
- Describe the purpose of the test – even if the learner knows it already, he will be relieved to hear that you know it too.
- Outline the tasks involved in the test.
- Mention the likely duration.

2.12.2 During the test:

- Take the opportunity, once or twice, to personalise the test to the learner. In an interview-type test, look for an area of common interest. If the learner does, or has done, something interesting or unusual, get him to talk about it. Everybody has a story to tell; it is a challenge to the interviewer to find out what that story is in a matter of minutes, just as taking a test in a foreign language is a challenge to the learner. Even if it's not a part of the fixed test procedure, a couple of minutes of personal conversation will help relax the atmosphere and encourage free conversation.
- Say something about yourself, too, if a natural opportunity occurs. Give the learner a glimpse of yourself as a person: your interests, your experiences, your opinions. You don't have to agree with him, just show him that you, as a human being, want to talk to him, as a human

being, and not just to process him as test fodder. Be prepared to become involved with the learner; how can you expect to get to know a person without some degree of involvement, however slight?

2.12.3   At the end of the test:

— Announce the end of the test.
— Leave the learner with a sense of accomplishment, feeling that he has done something interesting and learned something useful.
— Explain any deviations from procedure.
— Ask the learner if he has any questions.
— Give the score or result if it is appropriate and possible.
— Thank him!

3   Elicitation techniques

This chapter examines different oral test techniques in detail. There are more than sixty techniques and variations suggested here, only some of which will be suitable for a particular test programme. If you have read chapters 1 and 2, you will already have a good idea of which sort of techniques will be appropriate and which ones won't.

It may seem that there is little difference between some of the techniques: between Discussion and Interview, for example, or between Question and answer and Form-filling. In other cases, you could argue that one of the techniques is really a variation of another, or that a variation is a different technique in its own right. There is no natural classification of test techniques, so I have written the descriptions to make the similarities and differences as clear as possible to the user. This means that ultimately I have made arbitrary decisions about what to list as a separate technique, what to list as a variation of a technique, and what to leave out completely. The sensitive test designer will always want to adapt ideas to her own circumstances to produce the best test.

In some cases, it is apparent that the techniques call on other, more general, skills as well as oral proficiency: a general knowledge of the language, for example, or even general knowledge of the world. This is not necessarily a bad thing, and to some extent is unavoidable in tasks which claim to be authentic; such general knowledge contributes to the overall ability to communicate. The broad aim of all these techniques is to encourage learners to speak by giving them something to speak about; close attention to the design of the marking system will ensure that it rewards the oral proficiency and not the more general skills of the learner.

The order in which the techniques are listed follows, very roughly, a scale of increasing predictability of response, from the least controlled to the most controlled. Thus, Reading aloud (see 3.15) produces an entirely predictable response, while an Interview (see 3.5) is less controlled. Some kind of order is desirable, but this does not imply that techniques nearer the beginning are inherently better than ones at the end. Any one technique can only be more or less suitable for a particular oral test; the great majority of oral tests contain two or more elicitation techniques, with a balance between the more controlled and the less controlled.

3.1   Discussion/conversation

Technique

This is the most natural thing in the world – two people having a conversation on a topic of common interest. It is also the hardest to make happen in the framework of a language test; it can only occur when both parties are relaxed and confident and something sparks between them, allowing the activity (a conversation) to become dominant, and its ulterior purpose (a language test) to be temporarily subordinated. The oral test then reaches its highest degree of authenticity by no longer being a test.

To somebody outside the conversation, it is hard to distinguish from an interview (see 3.5), but the distinction is useful. The difference is one of attitude or intention, rather than technique: in a discussion/conversation, the interviewer keeps overall control, but is willing and able to yield the initiative to the learner to steer the conversation or bring up a new topic. More accurately, the topics discussed and the directions taken by the conversation are the result of the interaction between the people, involved in a kind of negotiation below the surface level of the words. Tone of voice, pitch and intonation, and expressions of face and body language all contribute to this negotiation. These are features of natural conversation which make this procedure, when it succeeds, authentic and communicative.

In practice, this success depends very much on the ability of the interviewer to create the right atmosphere, and it is a question of human personality; it has nothing to do with conventional testing. On the contrary, our inherited attitudes to tests, and the way they are usually conducted, hold learners away from us at arm's length and prevent this positive atmosphere. It is a challenge to the interviewer to create the right atmosphere in a very short time, just as it is a challenge to the learner to respond to it. When this happens an interview test suddenly becomes a human encounter, a meeting between two people. Usually, only learners with quite a high level of proficiency will feel confident enough to take the conversational initiative. Some oral test programmes will not want to offer the opportunity, in the interests of conciseness and comparability of language elicited.

Taking the initiative, asking questions, expressing disagreement, all require a command of particular language features. They can be learnt, like any other language feature. But they require also the kind of personality willing to do such things in a situation where you know you're being assessed: in other words, a willingness to take risks. Risk-taking can be deliberately encouraged as a language-learning strategy, as part of a programme to help learners to help themselves. However, a learner will only try to use it in a test if he knows that it will be considered positively, and not penalised. The natural instinct of many of us is to keep quiet, speak only when spoken to, and not to try to do anything clever. There is therefore a danger that a discussion/conversation technique will reward extrovert and talkative personalities rather than those who are less forthcoming.

This is to some extent inevitable; if you are willing to give learners the initiative, and expect them to start behaving as normally as possible, you should not be surprised when they do start behaving normally – i.e. differently. (Only in conventional language tests are people all expected to behave in the same way!) A lot can be done by the interviewer to even out this bias, by being as sensitive as she possibly can to the personality and behaviour of the learner. One simple rule is not to talk too much – be prepared to leave short spaces or longer silences for the learner to decide what to say, to think of the words or to summon up the courage to speak.

Features such as false starts, ambiguous statements, mumbles and shifts of focus of meaning are characteristic of ordinary conversation, and ideally learners should show their ability to cope with them; it is difficult to introduce them deliberately in a natural manner, but they should not be avoided by the use of 'teacherspeak' either.

Variations

How many variations of an ordinary conversation are there? There is a lot of scope for trying out different ideas to suit the local circumstances. For example, try variations on the time, place and people involved in the test.

Time: don't feel you have to stick to a fixed time limit. If the conversation is interesting, carry on; if it runs out of steam, finish early. But if it doesn't really take off at all, then it will not have been a satisfactory test, and some other technique should be tried.

Place: since no special equipment is needed, try holding tests somewhere ordinary – an office, a cafeteria, a lounge. The more natural the surroundings the less dominant the test aspect will be, and the more naturally the learner can behave.

People: try not to use a fixed appointment system. Rather than keep the next learner waiting, encourage him to come in and join in the discussion – people coming and going is another feature of natural conversation. If there are other people in the same room, bring them into the conversation as unofficial interlocutors.

3.2   Oral report

Technique

The learner prepares and gives an oral presentation lasting from five to ten minutes. He is expected to refer to notes, but reading aloud is strongly discouraged. The use of simple aids such as an overhead projector, blackboard or flipchart diagrams is encouraged if appropriate. At the end of the presentation, the speaker is expected to deal with any questions. Making presentations is an authentic and communicative activity both for professional and academic purposes.

In a formal test procedure, the learner makes the presentation directly to the interviewer.

In a less formal situation, mini-presentations may be a routine part of the daily teaching schedule and be used for testing purposes at the same time. Each day one learner in turn makes his presentation to the rest of the class who are expected to ask questions and discuss the topic at the end. When this procedure has been established, the whole activity, from introducing the speaker at the beginning through the presentation and question-and-answer session to a final summary, can be conducted by the learners without the intervention of teacher or assessor. The presentation may be taped either for marking or for subsequent classroom analysis.

Choosing the topic is very important. It should be relevant to the aims of the programme or the needs of the learners and should contain new information or put over a new point of view. It should not be so specialised that only the speaker himself is interested, nor should it be so general that it has no apparent purpose other than as a language exercise. Ideally, the topic should be chosen by the learner in consultation with his teacher who will help match the ability of the learner with the difficulty of a given topic. Some learners will play safe by choosing the topic they are most familiar with. However well-prepared a speaker is, he will not be able to talk as confidently about a new topic as he will about one he already knows well. The assessor has to be careful to take this into consideration: is the topic in itself a difficult one irrespective of the fluency of the speaker?

Marking

Particularly when giving presentations is an authentic activity for the learners, specific mark categories (see 4.5) can be used for the different functional skills involved, for example, explaining factual data, expressing opinions or arguments, dealing with questions, summarising, and so on. In this way, particular weaknesses can be identified for further practice.

Where the presentation is given to an audience, the assessor will be able to back up her own impressions by watching the effect the speaker has on the listeners in terms of their comprehension, their reactions, and their questions.

VARIATION 1: MAKING A MINI-PRESENTATION WITH LIMITED PREPARATION TIME

On a smaller scale, learners can be given a short list of topics ten to fifteen minutes before the oral test, and invited to choose one on which to speak for two minutes during the test. The subjects will obviously be general, but should be phrased so as to encourage the learner to express his own opinions on specific aspects of the topic. Thus:

> 'Do you agree with lower speed limits and the compulsory use of seat belts? Why?'

is a better topic than:

> 'What should be done to improve road safety?'

And:

> 'What do you personally think are the best ways to improve contacts between people in different countries?'

is better than:

> 'How can international understanding be improved?'

VARIATION 2: IDENTIFYING A TOPIC OF PERSONAL INTEREST AT A PREVIOUS STAGE

Instead of imposing a limited choice and formal preparation time on the learner, another way of eliciting a short presentation is to try consciously to identify possible topics in earlier stages of the test. For example, the oral test can begin with a question and answer routine (see 3.9) which deliberately asks about hobbies, professional interests, past experiences of different cultures, jobs, etc. Some examples of such probing questions are:

- What do you do in your spare time?
- What kind of books do you like reading?
- What did you do on your last holiday?
- Do you enjoy travelling? Where to? Why?
- If you could live anywhere in the world, where would you choose?
- Have you done different kinds of job in the past?
- Do you ever think of changing your job? What to?

The interviewer makes a note of these, and later asks the learner to speak for one or two minutes about a topic that has suggested itself, possibly to a second interviewer. The learner should of course know that he will be asked to do this; and the interviewer must be alert to the possibility of memorised speeches.

Making unprepared reports, even short ones, is going to favour some types of personality over others, such as shy people. Among native speakers, some people would obviously do better than others, one of the major factors being educational background. The advantage of this variation is that the interviewer deliberately tries to choose a topic that the learner knows something about, and is therefore going to be able to speak about with some confidence.

3.3 Learner–learner joint discussion/decision making

Technique

A group of two or more learners are tested together, without the participation of an interviewer. The learners have to maintain and direct the discussion entirely on their own. The task usually involves taking information from written documents and coming to a decision or consensus about certain questions through group discussion. Where several documents or sources are used, these can be read before the discussion begins, or even form a previous stage in a test battery (see 2.10, Sequencing test techniques). Since it is the discussion, rather than the final decision, that is the important feature, there is usually no single correct answer; otherwise, having reached a conclusion, the learners will tend to sit back and wait rather than continue talking. Learners are told beforehand that the assessment will be based on the way they express and justify their opinions, and evaluate those of others, and not just on the factual content of what they say. The discussion may be marked live or it may be taped for later marking.

Some examples of the type of tasks that can be set are:

— Choosing a suitable educational course for a person with specified interests.
— Choosing a suitable holiday for a particular person or family from brochures.
— Choosing the best bid for a contract from a number of bids.
— Choosing the best candidate for a job from among a number of applicants.
— Deciding which applications for bank loans should be granted, when the total amount of the loans requested exceeds the amount of money available.
— Discussing a proposal for a company (real or imaginary) to launch a new product or enter a new field of operation.

The literature made available may be authentic brochures, forms, etc., or may have been written for the purpose of the test. In either case, they must be kept simple and relatively short to avoid the test becoming one of reading comprehension. This documentation must be carefully chosen or prepared. The possibilities to choose from must be sufficiently numerous and different to allow room for discussion, while not offering any one obvious best choice.

This technique, and the variations below, give the learners considerably more control over what happens than is normally the case in the language classroom. It will probably be necessary, therefore, to practise holding free discussions as a regular part of the teaching programme; not just to acquire particular forms of language – although negotiating discussion points and reaching a consensus do use certain language functions a lot – but more importantly to get learners used to the idea of learner-centred work and independence from the teacher. Some learners will need encouragement to play a full part in undirected discussions, particularly if the subject holds no special interest for them. In order to help the discussion get going, the directions to the participants may contain a short list of factors that are to be considered, along with the instructions to 'justify your recommendations'.

VARIATION 1: DISCUSSING A TAPED MINI-LECTURE

A group of four to eight learners listen together to a tape, five to ten minutes in length, on a topic of common specific interest where possible, and general interest where not; for example, a radio news report on a current issue. The learners may take notes if they wish, but should not subsequently read or quote from them in large chunks. They then discuss the main points raised by the tape, collectively taking responsibility for choosing the particular topics to discuss and guiding their discussion accordingly.

There is no interviewer as such – there may be an assessor or observer present in the room to ensure that the instructions are understood and the tape is clearly comprehensible, but she may then leave the room before the discussion, leaving the tape-recorder with microphone running to record the discussion for subsequent marking. If she remains, particularly as an assessor, she should make every effort to remain as insignificant and unobtrusive as possible.

Without interviewer control, the amount different learners speak will vary widely – a reflection of the authenticity of the discussion. In classroom practice sessions, the problem of the shy speaker can be tackled to encourage him to speak more; but some participants will always talk a lot more than others (without necessarily saying anything new or more sensible!). The marking system must therefore be designed to reflect this, and not to reward the garrulous at the expense of the more succinct, or vice versa: any system that is based on additive (see 4.9) or subtractive marking (see 4.10) should be calculated as so many plus or minus points per ten utterances or per one hundred words.

VARIATION 2: DISCUSSING IDENTITY FROM PERSONAL
POSSESSIONS

A group of learners are given a number of items of small 'personal effects' of the kind a person regularly carries around in pockets, wallet, handbag or briefcase: tickets, business cards, photographs, letters, cheque stubs, receipts, address book, diary, etc. Their task is to discuss the various items and to try to come to some kind of consensus about the person concerned – his or her age, job, family status, interests, lifestyle and so on. This is particularly good for testing the language of hypothesis, conjecture and negotiation. As long as all the participants understand that they are not trying to find any 'correct' answer, and they feel relaxed and confident enough to let their imaginations go, this technique can be very productive and enjoyable.

3.4 Role-play

Technique

The learner is asked to take on a particular role and to imagine himself in that role in a particular situation. He has to converse with the interviewer in a way that is appropriate to the role and the situation given.

The learner is given a set of instructions, just before the test, that explain in simple language exactly what he is supposed to do. For more confident learners, these instructions may be expressed in terms of the general situation:

> Imagine you are a foreign tourist in Britain, and you want to visit Edinburgh. You are talking to a travel agent. Find out how to get there. Make your own decision about how to travel.

Or the instructions may be made more specific, to give the learner more direction and to elicit more comparable language from each learner:

> You are a foreign tourist in Britain. You want to visit Edinburgh, so you go to see a travel agent. After you have explained the situation, ask him how to get to Edinburgh. Ask about the price, the travelling time, comfort, etc., and ask his opinion. Decide how you will travel, and explain why.

The ability to ask questions is important in this particular example. This skill is often overlooked in oral tests, and it is something role-plays are good at eliciting.

Elicitation techniques

If learners are unfamiliar with role-playing, the procedure and purpose should be explained well beforehand, and the instructions for each role-play should be given in writing, in the native language if necessary. If she is in any doubt, the tester should check that the learner understands both the general procedure and the specific instructions. It is important that role-play does not become a test of comprehension of instructions.

Topics and situations

Role-play situations may be chosen to test the learner's command of general social language, or to elicit particular types of language. For example:

— Particular functions e.g. complaining, enquiring, giving directions.
— Particular structures e.g. narration of accident (past tenses); report of theft, break-in (passive); getting information (asking questions).
— Particular topics, vocabulary e.g. hotel or flight booking; ordering goods.
— Ability to circumlocute, to make oneself understood despite ignorance of specific vocabulary. The situations chosen for this will be deliberately unfamiliar.

The situations chosen for a role-play may be simple or complex.

A simple situation is a stereotype of an ordinary everyday event that the learner might easily find himself in, requiring the use of ordinary everyday language. The most straightforward examples involve the use of polite social formulae, and are effectively the same as in Making appropriate responses (3.8); but the simple role-play usually requires the learner to make a series of appropriate statements in one continuous role. The tester is both the narrator, setting the scene and linking the tasks, and a character in the role-play. For example, a learner might be cast in the role of a foreign visitor talking to a waiter at a café, ordering a drink, asking for local information, describing his needs, saying a bit about himself, persuading the waiter to accept a large denomination note, etc.

A complex situation has an added feature that is unusual, but not unlikely, in everyday life – an urgent message, an unexpected surprise or offer, a breakdown, a job interview or an accident; it sometimes involves a degree of suasion, getting the other person to do something that he does not want or expect to do. It may also involve the learner putting himself in a role that he has no experience of, for example, as a policeman, an information officer or a businessman.

Personal reluctance

A possible problem is personal reluctance to participate. Role-playing by definition implies pretending, even in a small way, to be someone other than you really are. Some people can do this more easily than others. In some cultures, role-playing may be seen as unusual and therefore unsettling behaviour, especially in an educational context. Some individuals are personally unhappy about pretending to be someone else, and any attempt at persuasion may only increase this unease. Therefore, there are both cultural and individual differences between people in their ability to role-play which do not reflect differences in language proficiency. If you think your oral test may run into this problem, abandon the role-play and use other techniques instead.

VARIATION 1: ROLE-PLAY BETWEEN LEARNERS

To avoid the inhibiting effect of the interviewer playing a role opposite the learner, learners can be paired together for a role-play. They are given written instructions a few minutes before the test; each learner in a pair being given a role, and perhaps a specific task to carry out, that is matched by his partner's role. Since the interviewer is no longer in control, and should only intervene in an emergency, the aim must be to set the situations clearly enough for the learners to be able to carry out their roles without further prompting, while keeping them open enough to allow for learner initiative and ingenuity.

Some examples of matching roles are:

— boy and girl meet at party
— journalist + politician
— lawyer + client accused of . . .
— policeman + member of public reporting missing person
— shop manager + person making complaint about goods
— detective + last person to see deceased alive
— hotel receptionist + tourist
— doctor + patient with a problem

Depending on the learners – their age, imagination, familiarity with role-playing – these situations can be specified in great detail in the instructions, or the detail can be left entirely to the learners to invent. If appropriate, the learners can make up the details between them. However, in order to balance out the language produced and the difficulty of each role, some instructions can give extra tasks, such as 'Ask at least three questions . . . ' or 'At the end, summarise to make sure you have understood what the other person has said.' Alternatively, at the end of the role-play the interviewer can call on either learner to give a summary, say what he would do next, or ask for more information.

These learner–learner role-plays are usually great fun. Learners tend to get very involved, with visibly greater spontaneity and creativity than in 'talking to teacher' role-plays. As it is sometimes difficult to stop them, a time limit should be clearly specified in the instructions.

VARIATION 2: USING A TELEPHONE

A telephone is a highly authentic medium for a role-play, as it is an increasingly important instrument for communication. It is particularly good for eliciting the language of checking, asking for repetition, spelling out names and places, as well as eliciting the language of making a telephone call. Using an internal telephone system makes it possible to involve other people in different roles in a way that would not be economical face-to-face. The learner's role may call on him either to initiate the phone call and to carry out certain tasks, or to respond to the phone call when it comes. In the latter case, he will have a general idea of what his role is – postman or politician – but will not know in advance exactly what the caller will say to him or the ostensible reason for the call.

3.5 Interview

Technique

The interview is the most common of all oral tests; for many people, it is the only kind of oral test. It is a direct, face-to-face exchange between learner and interviewer. It follows a pre-determined structure, but still allows both people a degree of freedom to say what they genuinely think. It therefore falls between two other techniques described in this chapter: 3.1 Discussion/conversation and 3.9 Question and answer. The distinctions between these three techniques are frequently blurred in practice; but they are worth making clear in principle.

Compared with 3.1 Discussion/conversation, an interview is structured. The interviewer sets out to find out certain things about the learner and to get answers to certain questions. She maintains firm control, and keeps the initiative as well; whatever the learner says is in more or less direct response to her questions or statements. However, the learner still has the freedom to answer as he likes, or to develop his comments and opinions. When he has finished his answer or his comment, it is then up to the interviewer to make the next move; to develop the topic further or raise a new one.

The questions and topics raised by the interviewer are chosen for their success in eliciting a representative sample of the learner's speech. Interviewers usually have a prepared list of written or memorised questions to ask, or topics to bring up. This mental or written list will contain quite a wide variety of questions and topics in order to avoid constant repetition and possible compromise. The final choice of topics and questions used will be left to the interviewer to decide during the course of the interview.

Compared with 3.9 Question and answer, however, an interview is more authentic; it has a consistency and a relevance that stretches over more than one question or comment. There may be several topics raised in an interview, but each is explored in enough detail, with follow-up questions and prompting, to allow the learner to develop it and to show his proficiency, rather than just giving a straight answer to a straight question.

Stages in the interview

An interviewer starts out with a deliberate plan. For a short interview of between five and eight minutes, this might be:

a) introduction (polite social questions to put learner at ease)
b) find level (series of questions and topics to establish level against a specific scale)
c) check questions (above and below the established level, to confirm that it is right)

For a longer interview of between ten and fifteen minutes:

a) introduction and warm-up
b) establish approximate level
c) fine-tune level – several more topics/questions at about the right level (and a little above) to offer the learner the opportunity to improve his rating
d) elicit learner's opinion (see 2.1):
   – on his oral ability
   – on his overall proficiency
   – on his own strengths and weaknesses in the language
   – and perhaps, offer the opportunity to correct one or two earlier errors (see 3.18)
e) feedback and wind-up: if possible, tell the learner the result; invite any comment; end the interview

The interviewer chooses her questions and comments to fit the purpose of each stage. When she feels the function of one stage has been achieved, she moves on to the next, trying to make the transition as smooth as possible.

In the earlier stages, the interviewer will take care to help the learner's confidence by filling awkward pauses, perhaps providing words the learner is searching for, glossing over major errors of communication, and speaking clearly. As the interview progresses, and the learner warms to the procedure, the interviewer should try to pull back a bit, and to give the learner more space.

In particular, the interviewer should be careful not to:

– over-correct errors (an instinctive teacher habit!)

- fill pauses or silences automatically
- interrupt unless necessary
- impose her own opinion unnecessarily

Interviews at higher levels

Oral interviews often fail to discriminate effectively at higher levels. The oral interview technique is well-suited for testing learners at the inter-mediate level and below, where detailed rating scales (see 4.7) present easily-recognisable learner profiles; but at higher levels it is difficult to produce such well-defined scales, and the usual mark categories (see 4.5) fail to discriminate well. The tightly-controlled interview that is more like a question and answer test (see 3.9) will not easily elicit the learner's best language performance, and it is therefore more important at higher levels that the interviewer stand back a little and allow the learner to display his conversational fluency skills. Filling conversational pauses naturally and correcting one's own errors (sometimes called 'self-repair') are two of the features that distinguish higher-level from intermediate-level learners. Ultimately, the interviewer must be prepared to yield the initiative to the learner, as is the aim in Discussion/conversation (3.1).

This gradual relaxation of control is something the interviewer tries to do consciously in the course of the interview. It will communicate itself to the learner, who can then demonstrate if he is able to respond. The inter-viewer should also try to get as close as possible to her natural speed and style of speaking, and to avoid using 'teacherspeak', that peculiar form of over-articulated English that is never heard in the outside world!

See 3.9, Question and answer, for different types of questions that can be used successfully.

3.6 Learner–learner description and re-creation

Technique

One learner describes a design or construction of model building materials to another learner who has to reconstruct the model from the description alone, without seeing the original. The first learner cannot see the reconstruction, so he does not know how successful his description is. The language used is rated for accuracy of description and non-ambiguity; the degree of success of communication may also be judged by the time taken to complete the model, or by the degree of accuracy of reconstruction achieved in a given time. The learners switch roles and repeat the task with a different model. The materials used can be any kind of building bricks or construction set ('Lego' is a firm favourite) or Cuisenaire rods. The greater the variety of sizes, colours and shapes available, the more varied the language elicited can be.

In its most simple form, this technique elicits language in one direction only – from the learner describing, to the learner constructing. In another version, the builder can ask questions to check or clarify the instructions. This is a good way of eliciting descriptive questions. Both of these versions can also be conducted over the telephone, if this is more relevant to the learners' needs or more convenient for the purposes of the test.

The model to be described can either be shown to the learner already completed, or it can be constructed in front of his eyes by the interviewer, with the learner describing each step as it happens. In this way, the interviewer can respond to the learner's language by changing the design as it goes along. This allows her to check particular features of his language and to offer him the opportunity for self-correction.

This is a good technique for generating and checking detailed description of physical objects; it requires a command of the language of colour, dimension, location in three dimensions and sequence in description. It can be used as a regular test task from a very early level without ever using the same model twice.

For higher levels of general proficiency, a greater degree of detail can be expected, such as 'about 1 cm from the right-hand end of the yellow rod' rather than 'near the end of the yellow rod'; or 'forming an angle of about 30 degrees to the black rod, but not actually touching it' rather than 'at an angle to the black rod'.

This task is communicative, in that both learners wish to transfer information accurately across the gap between them so that they may succeed in their joint task; it is authentic to the extent that we all need, at one time or another, to describe objects and talk about relative location. For learners needing work-related technical language it can be authenticated at a much more sophisticated level of description.

VARIATION 1: REPORTING DESCRIPTION TO PARTNER

In this version, learners work in pairs. One learner only from each pair can look at the original model in another room, and must then come back to report his description to his team-mate who builds the replica accordingly. The reporter cannot physically assist in the reconstruction, but he can give any verbal assistance he wants to, revising or expanding his description as he watches. The builder cannot himself go to look at the original, but he can interrogate his reporter to check any point of detail. Clearly, the non-linguistic skills of accurate short-term memory and spatial perception will also help in the performance of this task.

VARIATION 2: MAP-READING/THE TREASURE HUNT

One learner describes to another a pre-determined route along a map. The second learner has to follow the route along his own unmarked map, either tracing it with his finger, or drawing it in pencil. At the end of the description, he marks the final point clearly on the map. Street maps of real or imaginary towns can be used, and this tests the ability to give accurate and clear directions. To make the task easier, more street names and other reference points, such as named buildings, can be given. To make the task harder when the tracer is able to interrogate the describer, small differences can be introduced between the maps, such as a slightly different name or a missing detail.

VARIATION 3: COMPARING MODELS

The techniques above elicit a language description which is used as the sample for rating the learner's language proficiency. In each case, a further stage can be added to the elicitation procedure: the comparison by the learners of the reconstructed model with the original, and their opinions, prompted if necessary, about the reasons for any differences. The ability to identify and analyse errors in communication is a good indication of awareness of the language.

3.7 Form-filling

Technique

The learner and interviewer work together to fill in a form. The questions usually concern the learner's personal details, professional situation or language needs. Either the interviewer or the learner may actually write in the answers; if the learner does it, the test will take longer and the learner will obviously feel his writing as well as his speaking skills are being tested. Alternatively, the learner can be given ten to fifteen minutes to fill in the form before the oral discussion, when the interviewer uses the completed form as the basis for an interview-type test (see 3.5 Interview). In this case, the form-filling serves to elicit information that the interviewer can use subsequently for discussion.

The form used may be a genuine form already used for other purposes (e.g. enrolment, statistical data on learners, or part of a progress or appraisal system); it can be a modified version of such a form; or it can be specially designed for the purpose of the test. If it fits in with the administration of the teaching/testing programme, a modified authentic form serves two purposes – testing and administration – and at the same time clearly shows its authenticity to the learner.

This activity is authentic. Filling in forms is something we have to do quite often in everyday life (particularly where state institutions or official training programmes are involved). Sometimes we fill in the form ourselves, sometimes the official person we are dealing with fills in the form, asking questions that may need to be discussed before deciding the best way to phrase the answer.

Form-filling is also communicative in that it elicits previously unknown information for an apparent purpose (if you consider filling in a form to be a real purpose!). It allows the interviewer, as well as acting as recording clerk, to exploit the information for discussion purposes, to elicit narration or description, or to find areas of common interest. By directing attention to the form, the interviewer makes the test an opportunity for co-operation rather than competition; learner and interviewer work together to complete the form instead of the interviewer trying to catch the learner out with trick questions, and the learner trying to avoid them.

VARIATION: USING A QUESTIONNAIRE

This is a widely-used teaching technique. Compared to a form, which usually asks for factual personal details or history, a questionnaire asks about one specific area of personal tastes or preferences in some detail, such as food, drink, music, entertainment, TV programmes, sport, hobbies, holidays, etc. The interviewer normally asks the learner the questions (though this can be reversed later to check the learner's production of question forms). The learner should of course have some advance notice of the task – it is difficult to give detailed answers to unexpected questionnaires even in your native language. It should be conducted in a reasonably light-hearted manner, and if it succeeds in showing a more human side to the test situation, so much the better.

3.8 Making appropriate responses

Technique

The learner is given a number of short, unrelated situations that might occur in everyday life. He may be given the situations written out on a sheet of paper; the situations may be read out to him; or both of these. He is asked to imagine himself in each situation in turn and to provide what he thinks would be an appropriate spoken response. The situations are designed to be easily described and easily understood, and require an answer of one or two sentences at most. They are designed to elicit functional language, for example, to ask for information, to apologise, or to refuse an invitation politely. There should usually be two or three correct and appropriate ways of responding. If the learner does not answer, the interviewer should check that the situation has been understood, and must watch out for cultural misunderstanding.

Over the last ten years, the functional aspect of language – recognising when a situation calls for a particular type of response, and supplying it appropriately – has come to be seen as an important part of language proficiency. This technique aims to test this command of functional language directly, in a way that few other techniques can.

Marking

This technique needs an assessor with a native-speaker command of the language who can assess the appropriateness of a response. Marks are awarded on a simple scale such as:

0 – inappropriate or seriously incorrect
1 – relevant but not entirely acceptable
2 – appropriate and correct

A native-speaker assessor will usually have little trouble deciding immediately whether a response is appropriate or not. A prepared list of acceptable answers can be constructed from intuition and by trying each situation out, but it is not always possible to anticipate every acceptable answer. A prepared marking key (see 4.4) should indicate how complete an answer has to be to be considered fully appropriate: for example, if the learner is asked to respond to a situation in which he has accidentally knocked against somebody in the street, is it enough to say 'I'm sorry' or would we expect 'I'm terribly sorry, I hope I haven't hurt you'?

This technique is quick and easy to use; several situations and responses take only a couple of minutes to administer and mark. However, there are some problems:

– Great care is needed to produce situations which are unambiguous and to which only one type of response is appropriate.
– There is a danger of cultural bias, favouring those learners with backgrounds culturally similar to the tester/marker, against those with culturally dissimilar backgrounds.
– Many learners today are learning English as an international language, for communication with other non-native speakers. A test that assesses knowledge of British English social phrases, for example, may be inappropriate for learners who will rarely speak to native English speakers.

Much of the utility and pleasure of using language to communicate stem from its unpredictability and creativity. A teaching/testing method based on the functionally appropriate response, taken to its logical conclusion, denies this creativity by asserting that we use language in certain situations in which certain responses are appropriate, and others are not. The functional approach to language has taught us a lot, but like all theories, it can be taken too far.

VARIATION: MAKING FORMULAIC RESPONSES

The learner can be put directly in a situation calling for an appropriate response by the use of certain polite social formulae. For example:

'I'm sorry you had to wait so long.'   ('That's quite all right.')
'My name's John Smith.'   ('I'm Pierre Leclerc.')
'How do you do?'   ('Fine, thanks – and you?')
'Have you had a good weekend?'   ('Yes, thank you.')
'It's a nice day today, isn't it?'   ('Yes, it is.')
'Did you have any trouble finding your way here?'   ('No, none at all.')

These are all authentic conversational openers and can be used, as naturally as possible, in the introductory stage of any face-to-face oral test. A personal favourite of mine is 'How are you?' to which the answer, quite often, is 'I'm thirty-five' (or whatever the learner's age is).

3.9 Question and answer

Technique

This typically consists of a series of disconnected questions which are graded in order of increasing difficulty, starting with short simple questions, such as 'What's your name?' and 'Where do you live?' and working up to long and complex sentences such as 'If you hadn't been taking this test this morning, what would you have been doing instead?' (This is the type commonly known as a silly question, but if you do want to use a hypothetical conditional, it's notoriously difficult to work it in naturally!) In a live test, this order allows the optional cut-off (see 2.11.4) to be used once the questions have clearly become too difficult.

A good way to start can be to ask a direct question about the learner's opinion of his own level: 'How well can you speak English?' This can be the quickest test ever; if a person can answer that question well, and at some length, he can speak well. An experienced assessor can sometimes place a learner's level more or less accurately on the basis of his answer to this one question. At the very least, it should give the interviewer a rough idea of level (see 2.1 Self-assessment).

The fact that the questions do not usually depend on each other in a meaningful way – they do not usually develop as a conversation – makes this a suitable technique to use for a taped test in a language laboratory. Learners should know how long they have to answer and are explicitly encouraged to keep speaking for the full amount of time.

Elicitation techniques

There is an infinite range of possible questions. Here are some of the most mundane, starting with some easier ones:

– What's your name? Could you spell it?
– How are you?
– (How well) can you speak English?
– Do you like speaking English?
– What do you do? What's your job?
– Tell me a little about your family.
– Can you count up to twenty?
– Can you tell me the time?
– What's the date today? What day of the week is it?
– What's the weather like?

– Where/how did you learn to speak English?
– Tell me three things you did yesterday.
– What were you doing/where were you at this time yesterday/last year?
– Where do you work/live? Do you like it there?
– How long have you been working/living there?
– What do you like doing in your spare time?

– What will you do when you leave here today?
– What are you going to do for your next holiday?
– What are your plans for the future?

– Have you ever been to Britain/America/Europe?
– What foreign countries have you visited?
– When did you go there? How long did you stay?
– What did you see/do?
– Did you enjoy your stay/visit? Why/why not?
– What differences in lifestyle/transport/food/people did you notice?
– Would you like to live/work/go back there?

– Why do you want to learn English?
– Can you speak any other languages? How well?
– What is most important in learning a language?
– What is the best method of learning a language?
– Do you think you are a good learner?
– What are your strongest/weakest points in English?
– Do you speak English outside the classroom? Where/when?

In a live test, any of these could be worth following up in more detail; the interviewer should be alert and notice when the learner might have something more to say, if prompted. If time allows, a discussion (see 3.1) might develop.

Rather than being entirely factual, the questions can require some imagination and expansion, for example:

— You spent the weekend camping with some friends. What did you do?
— You've just inherited a few hundred pounds. What will you do with the money?
— If you could change to any other job, what would you choose to do and why?
— A friend wants to invest some money, and asks your advice. What do you say?
— What's the first thing you would do if you became President/Prime Minister tomorrow?
— What general career advice would you give to a young person today?

Question and answer is a very common general-purpose test technique, especially suitable for lower levels, and as an achievement test for learners who have been following a carefully graded structural syllabus. It is easy to choose and adapt questions to suit the level; if one question is not understood, the interviewer can move on to another. However, it is tester-dominated and relatively unauthentic; unlike 3.1 and 3.5, there is no cumulative conversational meaning.

VARIATION 1: USING DIFFERENT QUESTION TYPES

As a deliberate strategy, the interviewer may wish to pose questions of different types, such as:

— yes/no questions
— question tag questions
— either/or questions
— simple factual questions
— descriptive questions
— narrative questions
— speculative questions
— hypothetical questions
— justification of opinion questions

These are in rough order of ascending difficulty. Generally, who/what/ where/when questions are simpler than how/why questions.

VARIATION 2: GIVING CUES FOR QUESTION FORMATION

At all levels, it is important to check that learners can ask questions as well as answer them — asking and answering questions being the two most basic functions necessary for survival in a foreign language. The interviewer can simply say:

Now I'd like you to ask me a few questions.
Ask me about my name, job, family and interests.

Or she can give the learner written cues for question formation:

Name? Job? How long for? Married? Children?
What do/last weekend? What plans/next holiday?

VARIATION 3: NAMING

The usual kinds of questions that learners are asked require at least a minimal standard of self-expression. Where the learner's proficiency falls short of this minimum, he may still know items of English vocabulary and be able to produce them with recognisably good pronunciation. This is particularly true of school English, studied many years before and unused since. For some test purposes it will be important to make a distinction between absolute beginners with no knowledge at all, and false beginners who have retained a small memorised vocabulary.

'What's this called?' or 'What's the name of this in English?' is all that is needed to elicit such basic vocabulary. Where necessary, the question itself can be translated. The question can be applied to:

— current conditions: the time of day, the day of the week, the date, the month, the year, the weather;
— items of clothing: shirt, trousers, shoes, jacket;
— everyday objects: pen, book, paper, chair, door, window.

With planning, a wide variety of common objects can be made available. A good follow-up question is, 'What colour is it?' A more difficult follow-up question can be, 'What's it for?' or 'How do you use it?'

Another way of testing for rote memory of previous learning is to ask the learner to recite the names of closed sets, such as days of the week, months of the year, as many colours as possible, numbers up to ten or twenty.

See also 3.11 Variation 4: Vocabulary naming from pictures.

3.10 Reading blank dialogue

Technique

The learner is given a dialogue with only one part written in. He has a few minutes in which to read it through and prepare the missing lines. The interviewer reads through her part of the dialogue, with the learner filling in the blanks aloud. The aim is to give the learner a clear idea of functional meaning of the missing parts, without putting the actual words into his mouth.

A well-prepared blank dialogue is more than a series of questions to find answers for. Often, the interviewer's sentence following the gap also constrains the learner's choice of words for that gap:

A: Can you tell me how to get to the station?
B: ....

A: And where does the bus stop?
B: ....
A: Oh yes, I can see it.

The choice of words to fill the gaps can be quite open-ended:

A: What did you do at the weekend?
B: .... (*but requires use of past tense*)

A: What was the weather like?
B: .... (*requires some reference to weather*)

Or, it can be constrained completely:

A: .... ?
B: I'm thirty one. (*requires question about age*)

This technique is useful for getting the learner to ask questions.

As in the example above, the stimulus he is given is an answer for which he must supply a suitable question, rather than the usual pattern of 'interviewer asks, learner answers'.

At a higher level, blank dialogues can be constructed that require the use of more complex functions, such as suasion, excuse, polite disagreement, warning and so on. The length of preparation time to be given depends on the difficulty of the task. If the general meaning of the missing sentences is easy to identify, there is an argument for keeping the preparation time short: the assessor wants to know not only whether the learner can work out something suitable to say from the surrounding context, but also, authentically, how quickly he can do it.

More difficult dialogues need more time, as they have to be read carefully for the meaning of the blanks to be understood:

A: How would you like to meet for a drink on Saturday?
B: ....

A: No, that suits me fine. Let's make it Sunday lunchtime.
B: ....

A: Yes, of course, I'd like to meet him.
B: ....

A: Well, if he doesn't, by all means bring him with you.
B: ....

A: Don't worry, I'll make sure it doesn't happen again.

A blank dialogue like this needs an experienced assessor or a sophisticated marking scheme. Responses must obviously be appropriate as well as correct, but should not need to exercise great powers of imagination; there is a danger of penalising the learner who understands what is called for but has difficulty inventing a plausible context, and therefore cannot fill the gaps adequately.

3.11   Using a picture or picture story

Technique

Before the test starts, the learner is given a picture or sequence of pictures to look at. Then the interviewer asks the learner to describe the picture or story and allows him to speak freely. When the learner has finished speaking, or if he falters, the interviewer may ask questions designed to elicit particular information, perhaps about a point the learner has missed or not made clear.

As soon as an interviewer begins to ask questions, the learner will tend to assume that he is now only expected to answer questions and is no longer expected to continue his commentary. Usually, the interviewer asks general questions intended to elicit the learner's attitudes or opinions on a topic related to the subject of the picture, but not directly about it. This is a common way of leading into a discussion (see 3.1). Unless the test is intended to check vocabulary, any items that may prove difficult can be supplied (for example, in a small word list under the picture).

A picture or cartoon story usually consists of from four to twelve drawings telling a story which is simple but allows the learner to add his own interpretation about the people or events involved. The pictures are specially drawn for this purpose, to exclude objects or actions which are difficult to describe or are very culture-specific. A single picture is often a photograph not taken specifically for the test, but selected for the same reasons. In both cases, the pictures can be exploited at two levels: description of the people, objects and events, leading into an interpretation and discussion of the more general issues raised.

Visual stimuli are an economic and effective way of providing a topic of conversation without giving the learner words and phrases to manipulate and give back. It is an excellent way of beginning a sequence of test techniques, and can be used just as a warm-up, lasting perhaps one or two minutes, without any formal marks being awarded. Although there is some freedom of expression, the topic of conversation is fixed by the picture or story, and the learner chooses his own words within the subject area.

Advantages

a) A well-chosen picture makes a point, and a good cartoon has a story to tell: these can be easily understood as the stimuli are visual rather than written. Sophisticated topics can be quickly introduced. The learner's ability to speak about what he sees will not be limited by his poor reading comprehension.

b) Speech samples from different learners are directly comparable because they are based on the same pictures; virtually the same story or interpretation will be given. This makes it easier to judge which learners communicate best.

c) At the same time, the words used by a learner are not completely predetermined; there is still a lot of opportunity for personal expression and interpretation.

d) A good picture can be the stimulus that generates the confidence to speak and a flow of conversation. If this is its purpose, the picture can be abandoned as soon as this warming-up has been achieved.

Disadvantages

a) With a visual stimulus, there is a danger that the learner will miss the point of a picture or story, for personal or cultural reasons. A learner from a culture in which men regularly cook, for example, may not react much to a picture story in which a man is cooking for his wife on a special occasion and making a mess of it. He would find it difficult to say much about such a mundane story. A learner from another culture, however, might appreciate the intended humour better, and may therefore have more to say. Even if the first learner is not penalised directly for missing the point, he may get marked down for having little to say.

b) Unless vocabulary items in the picture are supplied, the learner who knows the names of only two or three crucial items will be at a strong advantage over those who do not. Even if the items are supplied on request, and marks not deducted, it is psychologically demotivating to have to ask for vocabulary before you begin.

c) Suitable cartoon stories are hard to find and difficult for an amateur to draw. Even deciding on a good storyline can be a difficult task. Particularly in situations where learners can and will discuss with each other details of the test, it may be necessary to find several alternative pictures or stories to use in rotation.

VARIATION 1: USING SEVERAL SIMILAR PICTURES
The learner describes one of a number of similar pictures, which differ only in minor but significant details – how minor the differences are

depends on the general level of proficiency. The interviewer does not know which picture the learner is describing and has to use the learner's description to decide which it is. In theory, this is a more communicative task.

Alternatively, the interviewer's pictures have letters or labels under them, but the learner's do not; the learner has to find out which label goes with which picture.

Another alternative is to use 'spot-the-difference' type cartoons which are found in a variety of magazines and newspapers. The learner describes the differences between the pictures.

The important point in the scoring of this kind of task is to assess the fluency and facility of the language generated, and not the learner's visual acuity. Some learners will notice visual differences more quickly than others, quite independently of their oral proficiency; it seems unfair to mark up such learners, and penalise others, by rewarding their speed of perception.

VARIATION 2: ORDERING PICTURES TO CREATE A PICTURE STORY

The learner is given a small number of separate pictures or photos, and invited to put them in order and to tell the story based on that order. There should not be a single correct order, and marks should not be awarded for getting the order right or wrong; the aim is to give more scope for the learner's creativity and imagination by giving him more control over the events he is describing.

VARIATION 3: USING LIVE ACTION

The learner is asked to describe what a particular person is doing – using a short video film (good for specific language areas such as technical English); using another person in the room or visible from it; or the interviewer herself can mime specific actions. This is useful for eliciting language at a low level, with simple actions such as eating, reading, dressing, making a telephone call, opening a door and so on.

VARIATION 4: VOCABULARY NAMING FROM PICTURES

As a simple test of vocabulary, learners are shown a series of pictures one by one and asked to identify certain objects by name. The most suitable items are low in frequency but broad in range of occurrence; such words as button, tap, toilet, soap, wheel, brush, handle, switch, plug, are part of everyday life but are not often talked about. For marking purposes, this can form part of an assessment based on general impression, or the number of items correctly named can be counted to give the score.

Alternatively, vocabulary naming can be made a speeded test: the number of items correctly named from a picture or a series of pictures in thirty seconds.

At a higher level, much more difficult items can be chosen to discriminate between near-native speakers and the merely advanced. For example: tugboat, handstand, candlestick, flowerpot, handrail, radio aerial, box office (note that these are all compound nouns); or examples of lexical areas such as tools, furniture, cooking equipment, sports and pastimes, animals, means of transport, fruit and vegetables, etc. With trial and error, it may be possible to assign difficulty ratings to various objects, making fine discrimination possible.

VARIATION 5: GENERATING DIFFERENT TIMES AND TENSES

Each picture in a series has either the *day, date* or *time* marked in one corner (small clock faces can conveniently be used for the time). This allows direct control over the tenses to be generated, and permits the elicitation of any desired tense forms quickly and with some degree of continuity. Alternatively, the day, date or time assigned to each picture can be indicated by using a separate clock face, diary or calendar.

3.12 Giving instructions/description/explanation

Technique

With minimal preparation, the learner describes, at some length, a well-known object, a system or an everyday procedure. The description is factual and the object being described either widely known or easily comprehensible. Choosing something that is familiar to everybody is a good way of getting the learner to produce connected discourse on a given topic but allows considerable freedom of choice of expression without requiring extensive preparation. This distinguishes it from Oral report (3.2), which requires more thorough preparation on a more specialised subject. Normally, the learner is given a list of between five and seven topics to choose from and a few minutes' preparation time. Some examples of suitable topics are:

– How do you make a good cup of tea or coffee?
– Describe a bicycle.
– Describe how to prepare a favourite dish from your country.
– Give instructions for using a public pay-phone.
– Explain how you would advise someone to look for a job.
– Describe how people in your country celebrate the New Year.
– How does the education system work in your country?

The choice of topics can make the task more or less controlled. A question such as 'Describe your favourite meal' would be less controlled as there can be a lot of possible answers; whereas 'Explain how you change a car tyre' has basically only a single answer (in content, but many different ways of phrasing it). The important feature of all these topics is that in order to be satisfactorily carried out they require the learner to express himself at some length – say, a minimum of six to eight sentences.

The interviewer should be aware of the possibility of memorised speeches being worked into topics to which they are marginally relevant. If these memorised segments are large – two or three sentences long – they should be noticeable as being either stylistically unusual or irrelevant to the topic. The instructions and the marking system should make it clear that marks are awarded only for what is relevant to the subject. On the other hand, if the memorised segments are short, i.e. phrase length, they will probably be unnoticeable, and should arguably be rewarded anyway if they increase the overall fluency.

This technique can be used in a language laboratory, allowing two minutes' preparation time and then three minutes' speaking time.

VARIATION 1: EXPRESSING PERSONAL OPINIONS AND ATTITUDES AT LENGTH

Learners are invited to choose a discursive topic to speak on at a few minutes' notice. These would usually be topics of current interest on which everybody who follows current affairs is presumed to hold an opinion. As well as explaining his own position on his chosen issue, the learner is invited to give reasons supporting his position; and when he has finished speaking the interviewer may ask questions to clarify a point or to explore further the arguments presented. Such exploration may naturally take the form of presenting opposing arguments and asking the learner for further comment or justification.

The aim is not so much to start an argument as to demonstrate the learner's capacity to use the language effectively to justify a position, and not just state it. Examples of topics are:

– How much can governments do to relieve unemployment?
– Do you favour the increasing use of nuclear energy? Why?
– What would be your first act as Prime Minister?
– Is enough being done by the West to help developing nations?
– Should big cities heavily subsidise public transport? Why?
– Do you think foreigners make enough effort to understand the culture and people of your country?
– Why do women do so much work and receive so little money?

It will be noted firstly that these topics require quite a good level of proficiency, and secondly that they invite the learner to make tendentious replies. If it is evident that a learner has found a subject on which he has extended opinions, and is keen to share them at length, then the interviewer should console herself with the thought that a generous language sample is being generated. She should also be prepared to take a more actively interrogatory role.

VARIATION 2: EXPLAINING JOB-RELATED OR ACADEMIC TERMS

For learners who need English for academic or professional purposes, the topics for explanation are chosen from a small number of specialist subjects. These should require extended description or explanation using professional terminology, but should not be so difficult as to become a test of technical knowledge rather than language proficiency.

Examples:

— Science students can be asked to explain the purpose and method of operation of a piece of equipment.
— Trainee technicians can be asked to explain how a familiar mechanical or electrical system works; for example, what are the most basic steps in car maintenance?
— Teachers can be asked how they would answer a student's question on a common problem area.
— Students of business can be asked to comment on recent financial or commercial news.

3.13   Precis or re-tell story or text from aural stimulus

Technique

The learner hears a short passage or story on a recorded tape. He is then asked to re-tell the passage or to summarise it. The instructions usually emphasise that it is the quality, rather than the quantity, of the re-telling that is important; and that as far as possible he should use his own words rather than try to recall exact phrases from the passage. These points should be reinforced by the marking system, which should reward good paraphrase and the reproduction of the principal points of the story or passage (see 4.4 Marking keys).

This technique exercises the short-term storage and recall of information. Although the texts are relatively short – perhaps six to ten sentences – they are clearly too long to be memorised completely, so the task calls on the comprehension–processing–production sequence of skills. As a mixed skill test, you would not use it if you were trying to test speaking only; but clearly, speaking is rarely used in real life without listening also being involved, so it is, in that sense, authentic.

Using a taped passage, rather than have the interviewer reading the text aloud, standardises the presentation and reduces the load on the interviewer if she is also acting as the assessor. It is difficult for an interviewer reading aloud not to speak to the learner's perceived level of proficiency, which will lead to the task being made easier for some learners than for others. With a taped stimulus, and clear instructions (preferably in writing) this technique can also be used in a language laboratory.

VARIATION 1: DISCUSSING THE CONTEXT

Leading on from re-telling or summarising, the learner is invited to speculate about the context of the situation heard on the tape. Who is talking to whom, when and where? Is the language formal or informal? What went before and what might be said next? Where does this passage come from – a play, a novel, a documentary programme, a personal reminiscence? This version can be personalised by asking the learner what *he* would do or say next; the passages used can be chosen or adapted to set the scene for an appropriate response question (see 3.8) and the first two or three questions used only to make sure that he has properly understood the situation. Follow-up questions can check how far he understands the particular nuances of the language used.

This kind of discussion allows the learner to display his sensitivity to social and cultural features of language as well as his own ability to explain them. Rather than a single, long taped passage, it is more appropriate to use several different short ones, some of which consist of short snatches of conversation.

VARIATION 2: PASSING THE MESSAGE ON

In this variation, a live interlocutor gives the learner a message that he is to pass on to the interviewer. The message may be short and practical:

> Please tell Mary that this room is being used for an examination this afternoon; ask her if she would mind finding another room for today only.

It may deliberately contain a number of specific details:

> Tell Mary that I won't be able to teach my usual Advanced Class on Wednesday morning as I have a doctor's appointment at ten o'clock. Could she teach it for me? She can phone me any time this afternoon, on extension 23, to check the details.

Or it can be a short joke, riddle or story. The use of a live narrator is more authentic; the learner has the benefit of a live narration, and the possibility of asking for repetition, but at the same time he has to give some of his attention to responding to the narrator, and may therefore find it harder to concentrate on the message.

The message may be entirely pre-arranged; it may be newly invented by the interlocutor and therefore entirely novel to the interviewer who really has no idea what to expect; or it may be generally familiar, but with different details each time, which can be checked after the test for accuracy of transmission by the learner. The message can be deliberately constructed with gaps, to see if the learner asks the interlocutor the obvious question: who, in the second example above, is the message-giver? What is her name? That message relayed by the learner as 'Somebody told me to tell you that she . . .' is unsatisfactory. (On the other hand, it seems a bit unfair to award a learner marks for his message-taking skills if he only came for an oral test!)

The message giving can be arranged in different ways:

a) The learner is given the message before the start of the test. A few minutes are allowed to elapse, either waiting for the test to begin or doing some other test activity, before the interviewer asks for the message.

b) The interviewer leaves the room, and while she is out, an interlocutor comes in with a message for her. Seeing that she is not there, the interlocutor gives the message to the learner and asks him to pass it on.

c) Where there is another person – an interlocutor or assessor – in the room while the test is taking place, the interviewer can excuse herself for a couple of minutes on some pretext, and ask the learner in her absence to ask the interlocutor for some personal details – her name, her job, her personal background, her interests. On her return, the interviewer will ask the learner to summarise what he has learnt about the other person. This is a good technique for testing question forms.

d) In a system where two different interviewers are used in different parts of the test, the first interviewer gives the learner a message to pass on to the second interviewer.

3.14 Re-telling a story from written stimulus

Technique

The learner reads a passage or series of short passages to himself and is asked to re-tell each one in his own words immediately afterwards. There is no fixed time limit on the reading stage, but he is not allowed to refer back to the written text once he has begun to re-tell the story or text. Thus the learner is usually given the text to read at the beginning of this stage of the test, and the text is taken back by the interviewer once the learner says he has finished reading it. In this case, the recall is immediate. Alternatively, it is possible to delay the recall by carrying out some intervening activity between the reading and re-telling stages in order to accentuate the importance of memory and mental organisation.

This technique can be used at all levels. At lower levels, it may be necessary to offer help with vocabulary and to check understanding, so that the success in re-telling is not just a reflection of the degree of comprehension but as an authentic activity it necessarily involves comprehension and processing skills as much as speaking skills.

At elementary and intermediate levels, to discourage parrot-like repetition of words and phrases and to reduce the importance of memory, instructions can be given to keep the re-telling brief by reproducing only the most important points. This can be reinforced by the marking system: a marking key (see 4.4) awards marks on an additive basis (see 4.9) for each main point mentioned, and a mark or half-mark is subtracted (see 4.10) for each error likely to cause misunderstanding.

At higher levels, emphasis can be given (in preparation, instructions, and in the marking system) to the use of conjunctives and other sentence-connecting devices, particularly to reward the correct insertion of words not in the original text. Accurate and natural use of this discourse vocabulary is a skill that distinguishes fluent speakers from advanced learners who have a strong but largely passive command. With the passages selected and the marking key designed specifically to make this discrimination, this technique can be very useful at advanced levels.

The principal difference between this technique and 3.13 Re-telling from an aural stimulus, is, obviously, that the skills used are hearing/speaking in one case and reading/speaking in the other. Both are authentic, but for any particular learner the text types are likely to be different – in terms of subject matter, length, degree of formality, conversation or text, etc. This would naturally be reflected in the different passages chosen for each technique.

Another difference is that a taped passage is heard in real time, that is to say, the timing of the delivery is predetermined and the learner has no control over it. He has to process it as it comes. Access to a reading passage is much more under the learner's control; he can take it at his own speed, re-read phrases or sentences and refer back to check references. A written passage may therefore be linguistically more complex than a taped passage without the learner's ability to speak about it being impaired by poor comprehension.

VARIATION 1: USING NOTES

Particularly for academic purposes, learners can be asked to produce a short exposition or description from prepared note cards. All the learners start with the same written prompts, so they are being tested on the language they use rather than on their specialist knowledge. This is suitable, for example, for reconstituting and comparing different theories or explanations of data.

More generally, skeleton notes can be used for mini-presentations, anecdotes or narration; the notes give any special vocabulary and by providing the framework do not penalise less imaginative learners. They can be arranged in such a way as to test the use of connectives and discourse features.

VARIATION 2: USING A SET TEXT

Where the learner has read a set text, the interviewer shows him a paragraph or short section of it and asks him to explain its significance, or where it fits into the general storyline. Such questions are not intended to test either the learner's memory or knowledge of the book, or his instant comprehension; the aim is rather that they give him the opportunity to speak at length on a familiar subject. The interviewer may then ask more open-ended questions about, for example, the learner's favourite character in the book, or his overall opinion of it.

VARIATION 3: USING AN UNSEEN TEXT

The learner has a few minutes before the test to read a short text that he has not seen before. The interviewer can ask check questions about the meaning of the text or of words in it. Specific questions can be asked about discourse references between sentences in the text: 'What does *it* in the third line refer to?' Such detailed questions will clearly test reading comprehension as much as oral ability; this mixture of comprehension and speaking skills may be a deliberate and authentic feature of the test. Otherwise, not knowing one or two key words may cause a learner great difficulty and anxiety. The interviewer can avoid this by asking the learner if there are any words or phrases he has not understood.

Unseen texts can also be used as a springboard for speculation – since the text is previously unknown and unseen, what does the learner think might have happened before, and what might happen afterwards? What could the relationship be between two of the characters? Why might one of them have said or done something particular in the passage? Rather than the usual right-or-wrong interrogation, such questions allow a kind of negotiation to take place between learner and interviewer in a more relaxed atmosphere – that is if the interviewer can make it clear that she is not after a single correct answer.

3.15   Reading aloud

Technique

This technique requires the learner to read aloud to the interviewer, either a passage of text, or part of a dialogue in which the interviewer or another learner reads the other part. The learner is given the script five to ten minutes before the test to allow him to read through it and prepare.

Two or more passages can be used. In this case, the passages can be of different types – specialised technical or academic English as opposed to a general descriptive passage, for example – to widen the variety of language used. If test security is of great importance, several similar passages can be used and one or two allocated to each learner at random.

Advantages

a) The passages can be chosen according to the style, topic and difficulty of language desired. Precisely the language that is wanted can be generated.
b) Where the same text or texts are used for all learners, there is complete standardisation of what each learner says, and therefore greater comparability for the purposes of assessment and greater reliability of scores. Where different passages are used, they can be edited or reworded to make them as comparable as possible.
c) These techniques are simple to administer and quick to mark. Learners easily understand what is required of them.

Disadvantages

a) These techniques are not authentic; we rarely read a text passage aloud in a foreign language, and never read a written conversation aloud. Neither are they communicative; nobody is saying anything new to anyone else.
b) Good performance depends to a large extent on reading skill. This will clearly be important if the learners are likely to have differing degrees of literacy in the foreign language, or if as a group their reading skills are less well developed than their speaking skills. Reading aloud is a special skill in itself, in which great improvements can be made in a short time by specialised training, which has nothing to do with oral proficiency.
c) Even fully-literate adults will vary in the degree of confidence with which they can read aloud from a written text, even in their native language, partly because the instant feedback we get in normal conversation is lacking.

This technique is suitable for assessing the mechanical skills of language production such as pronunciation, intonation, word and sentence stress patterns. However, as well as testing mechanical speaking skills, these techniques also call on the ability to add meaning at the sentence and discourse levels. This is a kind of fluency, although it is harder to mark; but it is usually clear to the assessor if a learner is able to pronounce each word correctly in its isolated form but is unable to put the words together to form a stream of meaningful speech. The few minutes' preparation allows the proficient student to pick out the features that carry extra meaning, such as sentence-stress and intonation patterns. Correct production of these features suggests a good comprehension of the passage as a whole, and the ability to express more or less subtle shades of meaning. To make the most of these features, a detailed marking key (see 4.4) can be prepared for each passage.

VARIATION 1: READING SCRIPTED DIALOGUE, WITH SOMEONE ELSE READING THE OTHER PART

Reading one part in a dialogue adds an element of interaction, of a limited kind; the student is speaking to, and with, another person in the foreign language, although the conversation is wholly predictable. The participation of someone else helps the learner's confidence, as he is not entirely alone in the performance. If the other person is a native speaker, the way she reads her part is important. She can make the dialogue come alive by being interested, and if the learner is proficient, he can respond in the same way.

VARIATION 2: READING TEXT WITH PHONETIC MARKERS

A number of marker or key features – sounds, words or phrases – are chosen for testing, and a text is constructed that includes these features. The assessor has a list of these key features, and awards marks on the basis of how well they are produced. Although she is assessing performance on the basis of these pre-selected items, they are produced in the context of connected discourse.

These items can be selected to cover any particular area desired, such as technical vocabulary; idiomatic or conversational expressions; 'stream-of-speech' features such as assimilation, liaison, or contractions; words or sounds that are known to cause problems for speakers of a certain language; and so on.

VARIATION 3: READING SENTENCES CONTAINING MINIMAL PAIRS

This is a quick and easy way to test production of minimal pairs. These are sets of two or more words that differ in pronunciation only by a single sound, such as 'bear' and 'pear' or 'hit' and 'heat'. Learners often find it difficult to discriminate between these, particularly if a sound distinction does not exist in their native language.

In preparation, the learner is given a sheet of paper with a number of sentences written on it. Each sentence contains a minimal pair of alternative words each of which should be grammatically acceptable as well as semantically feasible. For example:

- The thing I enjoy most of all is working/walking.
- Try not to heat/hit the pan too much.
- The doctor's given me a bill/pill.

For each sentence, the learner chooses which of these words he is going to read out, and underlines it. Then in the test itself, the learner reads out each sentence aloud using the word he has underlined, and the assessor, as she listens, underlines the word she hears on a similar sheet of paper.

Subsequently, the two sets of sentences are compared – one with the words the listener intended to produce and one with the words the assessor actually heard – and the differences between them can be noted very quickly. This test would typically be used either after a period of tuition in which pronunciation had been consciously worked on, or as a diagnostic test to find out which pronunciation features need particular attention. It would be unwise to rely heavily on this alone as a test of pronunciation as there is a 50% chance of getting each answer right.

VARIATION 4: SPELLING ALOUD

The learner spells words aloud, letter by letter. At a low level, this checks his knowledge of the alphabet, and at a higher level it can be used for special-purpose tasks where accurate spelling (often of unusual personal or place names) is essential – for travel agents and telephonists, for example.

VARIATION 5: READING FROM A TABLE

Similar to variation 4 (above): the learner is asked to read aloud from a table containing only figures, letters, abbreviations, or initials in different quantities and units; or a text containing references to speed, weight, distance, and time, with their abbreviations embedded in the text.

To some extent, this is a generally useful skill; the ability to process abbreviations and pronounce figures accurately is necessary to all of us, but particularly for people who will use technical language – scientists, engineers, some academics and students – where accuracy of production and comprehension is essential.

3.16   Translating/interpreting

Technique

Both the interviewer and the learner have in front of them a native-language text with which the learner is familiar. The interviewer chooses a short passage, or series of passages, from the text and asks the learner to translate it into the foreign language. In the marking system, attention is paid both to the accuracy and correctness of the translation and to the style and feeling for the original. Familiarity with the content of the passage is essential if the learner is expected to be sensitive to nuances of style and register.

Translation is often regarded as old-fashioned and unsuitable for use in programmes where so-called direct method teaching is used. Translating well is a different skill from speaking well in the foreign language. It clearly requires interviewers or assessors who are at least fluent in both languages, and is therefore unlikely to be feasible for multi-lingual programmes. On its own, it does not make a satisfactory test of oral ability.

However, it is a quick and easy test to administer, and can conveniently be planned into a sequence of test techniques. It can follow on naturally from reading aloud (see 3.15) and lead into re-telling a written story (see 3.14). Although a teaching programme will probably aim to get learners to think entirely in the foreign language, and not translate all the time, interpreting or translating tasks are very authentic and can be made communicative.

VARIATION 1: TRANSLATING IN BOTH DIRECTIOINS

In this version, the learner acts as a bilingual interpreter who communicates between the interviewer and another person – a second interlocutor, an assessor or somebody on the telephone. One person assumes the role of a monolingual speaker of the learner's mother tongue, and the other the role of a speaker of the target language only; the interviewer asks the learner to pass messages or ask the other person a series of questions in the appropriate language and to translate the answers. This interpreter task can be made easier or more difficult by making the questions or topics more or less general and discursive, and the answers longer or shorter.

With more preparation, this can be used as a kind of role-play (see 3.4). The interviewer and the other person adopt particular roles which may conflict or require resolution, and the learner has to mediate or negotiate between them. For example:

– a tourist unable to understand the directions of a native
– a native landlord complaining about the noise a foreign tenant is making

- a foreign visitor who does not understand the bureaucratic procedure that a native official wishes to carry out
- a foreign customer at a post office
- a dissatisfied customer in a restaurant

This is highly authentic and an excellent test of oral ability. However, it needs to be carefully prepared, and the marking system must be very carefully thought out. Where the aim is to test the transfer of information from one language to the other, the marking scheme will reflect accuracy of translation. On the other hand, if the aim is to test the learner's ability to promote understanding between two people who are mutually unable to communicate, then learners' responses should not be marked only on word-for-word translation. Indeed, in some cases exact translation might well cause offence, and marks could be awarded for conciliatory mis-translation, and for adding comments that help to ease and clarify the situation.

VARIATION 2: TRANSLATING AN UNPREPARED PASSAGE

In this test of spontaneous translating, short paragraphs of three to five sentences on topics of current interest are taken from newspapers or magazines written in the learner's native language. The passage selected is given to the learner who is allowed only a few moments to read through it before giving a translation into the foreign language. The emphasis in this test and in the marking system should be on getting over the gist of the passage; a marking key (see 4.4) can be prepared with a list of key points to be scored. Several such short passages may be used; the first one to get a rough idea of the level and subsequent ones at a higher or lower level to zero in. This might naturally lead into a discussion of the different points of view of the native and foreign media to a particular topic.

VARIATION 3: TRANSLATING TEST IN THE LANGUAGE LABORATORY

Hearing a disembodied voice through headphones, and being expected to make an immediate and spontaneous translation, is a difficult and unnatural task. It can be made more 'friendly' by contextualising it, for example by setting up mini-situations which are described in writing in the learner's first language. The learner is given time to read each situation – only one or two sentences long – and then hears an appropriate response, also in the first language, which he has to translate into the foreign language.

Alternatively, the task can be set up as a recorded dialogue. The learner reads, and hears, a dialogue in which one part is in the foreign language, and the other part consists of responses in the native language; he hears the dialogue played once through, and the second time there is sufficient time after each native-language response for him to record his translation. For example, the script might read:

A telephone call at the office

Caller: Hello, is that the Office Equipment Company? (*in the FL*)
You: Yes, that's right. Can I help you? (*pause for translation*)
Caller: Can you tell me if you rent micro-computers? (*in the FL*)
You: Yes we do, but what make are you interested in? (*pause*)
Caller: I'd like to hire an IBM Personal Computer. Can you tell me how much it would cost? (*in the FL*)
You: We do rent IBM machines; can you tell me how long you would want it for? (*pause*)

and so on.

VARIATION 4: TRANSLATING DISCONNECTED WORDS OR PHRASES

Either live or in the language laboratory, the learner is given a written list of short sentences, phrases or individual words to translate. These can be chosen from:

— common social phrases or functional language
— well-known areas of language interference (false friends)
— a particular syllabus
— special needs vocabulary or vocabulary frequency lists

A large number of such items can be given and scored very quickly.

3.17 Sentence completion from aural or written stimulus

Technique

A series of sentences is prepared, for example in dialogue form, with the last few words missing from each. The interviewer asks the learner to read through the sentences, one at a time, and suggest a possible way of completing each one. Some preparation time can be given if desired, but for oral ability it may be better not to allow preparation. This can be done in a language laboratory, but a live interviewer can ask for repetition or elaboration if the learner has misunderstood the cue.

VARIATION 1: USING WRITTEN TESTS

Conventional written tests, such as cloze or multiple choice, can be used as the stimulus. The interviewer indicates a particular question and asks the learner to give the correct answer. The questions can be chosen to test knowledge of particular structures or vocabulary items; or the interviewer can choose different questions for each learner to prevent the test being compromised. The advantage of doing such a test orally is that it offers the opportunity for self-correction and allows the interviewer to find out why the learner chose a particular wrong answer; it is therefore a suitable technique for diagnostic testing.

VARIATION 2: USING GAPFILL TO CHECK DISCOURSE REFERENCE

A gapfill test can be used specifically to check the learner's understanding and command of discourse level reference. A text is chosen that contains a number of discourse references, such as pronouns, relative clauses, comparatives and features of substitution and ellipsis. The chosen words are deleted, and used as test questions for the learner to supply. (The most simple words, such as 'it' and 'that', are often the most difficult to explain, as there can apparently be several possible referents, including whole clauses as well as single nouns.) As an extension of this exercise, the interviewer can ask the learner to explain why he chose a particular answer, and to say which other words or phrases constrain the choice of answer to that question. Rather than just testing the ability to analyse discourse reference, the aim is to create the opportunity to speak and to use the language for a purpose, and this would be reflected in the marking key.

The use of conjunctions can be tested by giving two sentences from a text and asking for the most suitable word to join them: this can also be done at a lower level by giving a choice of connectives such as *because*, *but* or *then*; which word could you put between the sentences?

VARIATION 3: TEXT COMPLETION

The same skill of using discourse reference can be tested in a more open-ended way. Instead of filling gaps of a single word, the learner is asked to read a sentence, and to suggest another sentence that could precede it. The stimulus sentences are carefully prepared to require comprehension and production of discourse reference markers.

Some examples at different levels of difficulty:

- Nobody knows why.
- There's another one on the table.
- I'm not sure which to do first.
- However, it all turned out well.
- This decision will cause a lot of protest.
- Before doing this, check that the machine is not switched on.
- The risk is greater if your diet is not well-balanced.
- He gave other reasons which were more convincing.

VARIATION 4: USING SPOKEN CUES

The interviewer speaks the sentence to be completed, saying 'How would you complete this sentence?' and then gives the cue 'I'm sorry, I can't see you on Friday, but . . . '. This is more difficult than with a written cue.

If the interviewer accepts the learner's first answer, marks it right or wrong and moves on to the next question, the learner learns nothing from the process and might as well have taken an ordinary written test. It is much more useful if the interviewer allows the learner to make a second attempt, or to correct himself; this gives a lot more information about his control of the language. Particularly where there is more than one possible answer, but only one that is fully suitable, this can lead to a discussion about why one word or answer is better than another. This is a good way of testing sensitivity to subtle distinctions of register, nuance and idiom.

VARIATION 5: COMPLETING A WELL-KNOWN SAYING

The interviewer tells the learner the first few words of a well-known saying or idiom. The learner has to complete it. This is a high-level task that requires considerable familiarity not just with the language but with the culture as well. It would be inappropriate for learners wanting to use English as an international language, for example, but would be a good way of discriminating between people who have lived in an English-speaking country and those who have learnt only formal English. Some examples:

— You're putting the cart . . .
— No news is . . .
— It's like searching for a needle . . .
— Someone's been pulling . . . (2 possibilities)
— He's laughing all the way . . .
— Don't look a gift horse . . .
— That's adding insult . . .
— With the best will . . .

Warning! On its own, this technique tests only familiarity with certain idioms. There is considerable danger of such phrases falling quickly out of use; the life expectancy of a modern idiom may be only a matter of years. Pre-testing on native speakers is strongly advised, and a marking key to help assessors with nearly-correct answers is a good idea.

3.18 Sentence correction

Technique

The learner is presented with a sentence, orally or in writing, which contains an error. The task is to identify the error, i.e. say what is wrong, and to correct it. The errors may be of different kinds, graded by level of difficulty: grammatical errors such as concord, tense, choice of preposition or word order are relatively easy, other errors such as use of idiom or collocation are more difficult.

A passage with several errors, ranging from slight to severe, can be used instead of a single sentence. There might be no errors at all in a particular sentence. Where an error is one of usage, the learner can be invited to offer more than one possible correction, and discuss the circumstances in which one might be more appropriate than another.

Here again, the object is to provide a springboard for speech, and not just to see if the learner can correct errors. Finding and correcting errors is in any case an authentic task, particularly if you don't know whether there are any errors in the text.

VARIATION: CORRECTING YOUR OWN ERRORS

Offering the learner the opportunity to correct his own errors is something that can be done in the course of more or less any oral test; it doesn't have to be a separate stage. The danger of overuse is that the learner will start to monitor his speech much more closely, and become less willing to speak when, for example, his fluency is being tested. The interviewer can casually make notes of particular errors made by the learner in the course of the test, and at the end, present him with one or two to see if he can correct them immediately. This must be done in such a way as not to demoralise him!

3.19 Sentence transformation

Technique

The learner manipulates sentences to demonstrate knowledge of specific language structures. He is given a stimulus sentence, usually in writing, and is asked to transform it into a different grammatical pattern. The pattern desired is usually expressed by example, rather than by linguistic name: rather than say, 'Change this sentence into the passive' the interviewer should give an example and then say, 'Change this sentence in the same way.'

Commonly-used language laboratory drills can be used, two or three written examples leading into any number of tense or concord changes, active-passive transformations or sentence-joining tasks. As well as such general structural patterns, questions can be designed to elicit very specific language forms using the format: 'Rephrase this sentence with the same meaning, but beginning with these words . . . ' For example:

> The operator should check the machine settings, and he should also close the safety guard.
>
> As well as ....

This kind of activity is neither authentic nor communicative, but it does allow rapid testing of particular structural areas and an estimation of the learner's ability to correct himself.

VARIATION 1: REPORTING SPEECH

A more natural transformation task is asking the learner to report the speech of one person to another. The learner has a short conversation with the interviewer, and reports it to someone else, either one sentence at a time or in longer chunks – this encourages and tests automatic editing and rephrasing as well as direct reporting. This can be used to report questions and commands as well as statements. Tasks can vary from neutral requests for factual information ('Please ask what time the plane from Rome arrives.') to emotionally-charged situations ('Find out why he's so late!') in which the learner must use his knowledge of appropriateness as well as correctness. The marking system can be adjusted to reward this sensitivity to register. For example, the stimulus:

> 'Tell him to come and see me at four o'clock.'

would be literally reported as:

> 'Go and see him at four o'clock'.

But it would normally be preferable to say:

> 'Would you be able to see him at four o'clock?'

or:

> 'Do you think you could see him at four o'clock?'

VARIATION 2: REPORTING VIA THE TELEPHONE

Using a telephone for the direct or reported forms makes this activity more natural. In both private and professional life it is quite common to act as a relay between one person present in the room and another at the end of a telephone line.

The stimuli to be reported may be a series of disconnected sentences, or a longer utterance, which the learner must summarise and paraphrase; they may be on general or specific topics related to particular language needs. The direct form may (a) be given by the live interviewer to the learner, who then gives the reported form to the assessor down the telephone; or (b) the direct form may come from the telephone direct to the learner, who then reports it to the live interviewer. The skills of (a) initiating a telephone call in the first case, and (b) answering the telephone in the second, can also be built into the task and assessed.

3.20 Sentence repetition

Technique

The learner hears a series of sentences or utterances and repeats them as accurately as he can. The sentences may be read out by the interviewer or they may be recorded, which makes this a suitable technique for use in the language laboratory. With short and grammatically simple sentences, short-term memory and recall by imitation are often sufficient, but above a certain length, the learner must process what he hears, compare it with his internal grammar, store the information, and reprocess it for repetition. Sentence length can vary from one word ('Hello!') to fifteen or twenty words; sentences above this length are rare in natural speech, and difficult for most native speakers to repeat correctly.

This is a quick and effective test, which although neither authentic nor communicative, can discriminate well at all levels of ability. The easiest way to score is just to mark each sentence right or wrong, and to count up the number right over ten or twelve sentences; this requires no special training for assessors. Any scoring system which attempts to award marks for partly-correct repetitions is liable to become complex and hard to use. However, at higher levels and with longer sentences, where language processing is clearly involved, there is a good argument for rewarding repetitions which have the same meaning but employ different words or structures.

For example, if the stimulus sentence is:

He said he was hoping to come this weekend, but as it turned out he wasn't able to.

and the learner replies:

He said he was hoping to come this weekend, but in fact he couldn't.

that could be regarded as a fairly acceptable repetition. Rewarding meaningful paraphrase in this way would seem to make the test more valid, but involves a degree of judgement of acceptability on the part of the assessor that straight right-or-wrong repetition marking does not.

VARIATION 1: REPEATING SENTENCES OF INCREASING LENGTH

The sequence of sentences for repetition begins with one or two word utterances and the length progressively increases, one word at a time, until the learner gives a repetition which is clearly incorrect. Another sentence of the same length is given, and if that too is repeated incorrectly, the repetition task ends there (see 2.11.4 Optional cut-off). The number of words in the last successfully completed sentence can be used as the score. Quite a lot of trial and error will be necessary in the test construction process to get a variety of sentences which are, in practice, in order of increasing difficulty. Differences of familiarity of vocabulary and complexity of structure can make short sentences difficult and long ones easy.

VARIATION 2: REPETITION OF SENTENCES WITHIN SPECIFIC LANGUAGE AREAS

The sentences for repetition can be chosen or constructed to check comprehension and production of specific language areas, such as:

– structural or functional points covered in a syllabus
– specific items of vocabulary
– points of expected first-language interference
– phonetically similar words
– different stress and intonation patterns

A marking key (see 4.4) is prepared which rewards the correct reproduction of these specific features only, of which there are perhaps one or two in each sentence. This makes the test easier to mark as the assessor has only to listen out for these particular features, and mark each one as right or wrong.

4 Marking systems

The marking system is a vital part of an oral test. It must be integrated into the whole process of test design from the beginning; it is too important to be left to the end, as an afterthought. This chapter describes the most common ways to design and improve marking systems.

Test marking: the central problem

Objective tests types, such as a multiple-choice test, are very easy to mark. Only one marker is needed, and her judgement is never called into play. An answer is either completely right or completely wrong. One marker will give an answer paper exactly the same score as another, assuming they can both count properly. The consistency between markers, or *inter-marker reliability*, is very high. Similarly, if one marker marks the same answer paper on two occasions, two or three weeks apart, she will give it the same score both times. In this case, the *intra-marker reliability* is very high.

Tests that call for subjective judgement on the part of the marker, such as most oral tests or extended writing tasks like compositions, do not always have such high reliability. Either different markers give different scores to the same learner, or the same marker gives the same test (recorded on tape, for example) different scores on two different occasions. This poor reliability makes it difficult to be confident that the scores awarded in an oral test are accurate and trustworthy.

Two solutions

One solution, preferred by many language testers, is to avoid subjective tests altogether; and for some language testing purposes, such as grammar and comprehension, objective tests are sufficiently valid as well as being highly reliable. Administering and marking such tests is quick and easy; the only problem is that it gets terribly boring, with the ninety-third answer paper looking pretty much the same as the first.

For other purposes – testing integrative skills such as speaking or writing – objective tests are of more questionable validity, and a lot of time and effort has been spent devising objective test systems with credible claims to validity. In situations such as formal examinations, it is essential that the results should be as reliable as possible, and in such cases validity may have to take second place. In other cases, subjective and objective tests are put together in a single examination in the hope that it will combine the validity of the former and the reliability of the latter.

The second solution, and the one on which this book is based, is to make a conscious decision that the person-to-person aspect is so important in testing oral proficiency that it cannot be traded away, and to face up to the consequent problems of involving human judgement. People are inconsistent; they don't always agree, either with each other or with what they said or thought last week.

Having made this decision, the oral test designer now finds herself trying to devise a subjective, human testing system with credible claims to reliability. The key to this endeavour is the marking system, which becomes as significant as the test procedure itself. Just as much as the actual test, the marking system determines what has been tested. So the design of the marking system must be consistent with the aims of the programme and reflect the answers to all the other questions raised in chapters 1 and 2. At the planning stage, therefore, the test designer has to take great care over the selection and matching of oral test types and marking systems, and to design the system that best meets the needs of the learners and the aims and resources of the programme, while achieving the highest possible standard of reliability. This chapter looks at a number of ways to make the marking of subjective oral tests more consistent.

4.1   The number of assessors

The single most effective way of getting round the central problem of lack of reliability is to use more than one assessor. They may or may not be the same people as the interviewers. They may be present at the test, or they may mark from recorded tapes, or a mixture of these – one assessing live and one from a tape.

The hiccoughs or inconsistencies in the judgement of a single individual can be ironed out by combining her judgements with those of another person; the idea is that each person's hiccoughs are different so they tend to cancel each other out. So, two assessors, whose marks are combined, produce a more reliable score than a single assessor. Three assessors will be more reliable than two, and so on; but sooner or later you reach a point where adding an extra assessor doesn't improve the reliability all that much, it just adds an extra set of hiccoughs. This is the 'Numbers Paradox'.

The Numbers Paradox says that the more assessors you have for any single test, contributing to the overall score, the more reliable that score will be. However, the more assessors you have involved in the overall programme, the greater the problems of ensuring inter-rater reliability when different assessors are used for different tests.

The ideal solution to this is to have a small number of assessors, all of whom are present at every test. A more practical solution is to have just two assessors for each test, to select and train them as carefully as possible, and to make allowance for those occasions when a third opinion is needed.

The two assessors can have different roles – one can be the principal interviewer while the other sits back (literally, a bit further away) and listens. Perhaps she occasionally asks a question, makes a comment or helps things along. Then the assessors can change roles. One assessor can use the other as a partner for the learner to talk to – it feels slightly more natural to say, 'I'd like you to ask her a few questions' than 'I'd like you to ask me a few questions'. Or two assessors can conduct two different tests at the same time, and swap half-way through when they reach a certain point.

At the end of the test, the assessors either discuss their suggested marks and negotiate their way to an agreed score, or each writes her own mark down and they then take the average. Some provision should be made for calling in a third opinion. This would be done, for example, when there is a large discrepancy between the marks initially awarded by the two assessors; when the language produced by the learner seems atypical or insufficient; or when the learner himself feels that the mark he has been given is inaccurate.

If it is only possible to have one assessor, it is even more important to improve and maintain the consistency of marking. In such cases, the availability of a second opinion on demand is very desirable. The following sections make other suggestions.

4.2   The selection and training of assessors

Some people make better assessors than others. The marks they give tend to be more consistent, both with their previous marks and with the marks of other assessors. By setting up assessor training programmes and exercises, and setting standards of inter- and intra-marker reliability, you can make sure that you are using the best people available.

Such programmes should include discussion of the background and rationale of the test, but they should be primarily practical and lead the trainee assessor gently into an active role. Possible stages are:

– the background: the learners and the teaching programme
– the rationale: how and why the test developed
– linguistic and statistical aspects of the test procedure

— assess video-taped tests and discuss scores
— observe live tests with an experienced assessor
— take part in live tests, contributing to the score
— conduct live tests
— continue to take part in moderation exercises

The assessor training programme can be designed to train several people at a time, or just one or two. At the later stages there need not be a rigorous schedule; the trainee assessor should only proceed to the next step when she is confident she can handle it.

An example of an assessor training programme

Here is an example of a typical training programme for the selection and training of oral interviewers/assessors on the regular teaching staff at a large industrial training centre. The programme takes the form of a series of weekly one-hour meetings. Note how the staff who are going to use the oral test procedure are involved in its development right from the start.

Meeting 1:   all interested staff are invited to attend. The aims and problems of oral tests are outlined, including the principles of validity and reliability.

Meeting 2:   discussion of mark categories (see 4.5); which are desirable and which are actually realistic. Five broad categories are chosen: listening comprehension, vocabulary, accuracy, pronunciation, and communicative competence. These are subsequently defined in greater detail.

Meeting 3:   draft rating scales (see 4.7) are discussed using copies of several other scales as reference, taken from commercially published sources and standard reference books.

Meeting 4:   the broad test type (chapter 2) and the most suitable elicitation techniques (chapter 3) are discussed; a short-list of six tests is chosen. A sample, taped interview is played; some practical points of the general procedure for test administration and marking are considered.

Over the next two weeks, the assessors carry out a total of forty sample oral interviews, all recorded, at a variety of language levels and using the different techniques on the short-list.

Meeting 5:   personal feedback from sample interviews. The most common and most serious problems are identified and discussed; corrective action is agreed upon.

Subsequently, the test designer selects twenty of the taped interviews for rater-training on the basis of a range of levels, good sound quality, and the presence of typical problems (e.g. unclear or monosyllabic answers). These tapes are copied and their order randomised. Over the next two weeks, each assessor marks each of these twenty tapes, and all their marks for each category for each test are collated in a single table of results. To encourage frank discussion, each assessor is allocated a letter code.

Meeting 6:   the test techniques are discussed further and two are chosen: an interview (see 3.5) about the learner's job and talking about a picture (see 3.11). The average length is set at about fifteen minutes per test. The normal test routine is discussed.

Meeting 7:   the table of sample interview results is presented and discussed anonymously; nobody knows who the letter codes refer to. The average of all the assessors' marks is used as the norm. Major deviations are discussed in some detail; why do certain mark categories, and certain levels, produce a wider range of scores than others? Each assessor is subsequently told only which letter code represents her own marks, so she can compare them with the norm.

Meeting 8:   in the light of the sample tape marking, and the techniques decided on, the weighting (see 4.6) of the five categories is discussed and a decision made. The rating scales are reviewed.

The assessors are now ready to start conducting oral tests. Subsequently:

Meeting 9:   after a three-month period, each assessor re-marks five of the original twenty sample test tapes, as well as five newly-recorded interviews. The results of these are discussed, comparing each assessor with others (inter-rater reliability) and each assessor's original marks with her new marks for the re-marked tests (intra-rater reliability).

Meeting 10+:   the procedure for meeting 9 is repeated every three months, on each occasion using five old tests for re-marking and five new tests.

4.3   Marking recorded oral tests

Oral tests can be recorded on video or audio tape so that they can be marked later. This can be done as well as, or instead of, live marking. Taped tests are easier to mark because you can mark them when and where you want, and because you can rewind the tape and listen to what the learner says as often as you want. A common system is to have one assessor marking an oral test live and to have another assessor second-marking from a tape.

On the other hand, there is something important missing if you try to judge a person's communicative ability from a tape recording; it is partly the visual element that is missing, and using video instead of audio tape can help here. More importantly, if you are listening to a remote voice on a tape, that person is not talking directly to you and it is harder to judge how effective his communication is.

Marking from tapes is done for three reasons: as the first marking, where the test has been held in a language laboratory; second marking, as a check on the first marking of a live test; and re-marking tapes as an assessor-training procedure.

First marking of laboratory tapes

Where oral tests are carried out in a language laboratory, the tape marking is the first scoring procedure to be applied. Because there is no live marking at all, and therefore no possibility of asking the learner to repeat or say exactly what he meant by a particular comment, it is important that the tasks be as transparent as possible. In other words, the learner must be able to understand exactly what it is he is supposed to do, and the assessor must know exactly what the learner has done. Not only must the instructions be very clear, but the tasks themselves should be straightforward.

During the test, the operator must check that each learner is, in fact, speaking clearly, and immediately the test has finished, she should check that each tape has recorded to an acceptable level of quality. The time taken to mark each test from tape can be greatly reduced by test compression (see 2.8); this technique switches the learner's machine off when he is not actually speaking.

Total or partial re-marking as a scoring procedure

Re-marking from tapes as a routine scoring procedure can be done automatically for all the tests carried out, or it can be done for a proportion only. Using two live assessors is clearly better than one, but it may be too expensive or difficult to have two present at every test. Having the second assessor listening to the tape at some convenient time afterwards is often administratively easier to arrange.

If you do not have the resources to record and re-mark every single oral test, you can plan to re-mark a certain proportion only. The ones to be re-marked can be chosen:

– At random, choosing one in every five or ten tests.
– Depending on the first assessor's mark. For example all tests which were given a very high or very low mark by the first assessor; or all tests which are on a pass/fail borderline; or all tests where the marks seem inconsistent with marks gained on other tests.
– By request of the first assessor. However experienced she may be, there

will always be occasions when she finds it difficult to decide on a final score.

There are some grounds for saying that tape raters give lower marks than the original live interviewers. This might be because:

— They are not present at the creation of the speech sample so they are not directly involved in a live performance. They miss a lot of non-linguistic communication.
— Even with good recording equipment they may have trouble hearing and understanding some of the learner's utterances.
— They have more time to listen to a learner's errors, including the facility of play-back on the tape to check for further mistakes.
— Live interviewers follow their own style of interviewing and can gather their own evidence to make their assessment. Tape raters have to rate on the basis of someone else's technique.

If only some tapes are to be re-marked, it would be worth checking that their scores are not being consistently lowered by such factors, compared to the tests that are not re-marked.

Re-marking tapes as a rater-training procedure

Tapes can also be re-marked as part of an assessor-training procedure (see 4.2). A bank of taped oral tests is built up to be used either for individual assessors to re-mark after a period of time, or for a group of assessors to mark a number of tests together and compare their results. The individual re-marking aims to improve intra-marker reliability, and the group re-marking aims to improve inter-marker reliability.

4.4 Marking keys or marking protocols

In the world of diplomacy, a protocol is a set of established procedures that is to be followed on occasions when important people such as heads of state or government ministers meet. It tells people in advance what they are to do, step by step, and thus saves time and uncertainty.

A marking key or marking protocol has the same aim: to save time and uncertainty by specifying in advance, as far as is possible, how markers should approach the marking of each question or task.

For test procedures which follow an invariable routine, such as tests administered in a language laboratory where the learners respond to the same stimuli in the same order, the process of marking the test can be made quicker and more reliable by drawing up a detailed marking guide that tells the marker how to mark each question. For more open-ended tests, which are less predictable, a marking key must be more general, but can still be a useful guide to the marker.

A comprehensive marking key or protocol aims to:

— Anticipate problems that the marker is likely to face, and suggest how to cope with them.
— Maintain the aims of the test (see 1.1) by directing the marker's attention to the language areas that are most important, and by giving general guidelines for dealing with unusual responses.
— Describe the purpose of each question/task. The marking key should be written by the person or people who set the tasks. The more clearly the marker understands the test designer's intention, the better she will be able to deal with unexpected answers.

In order to anticipate problems successfully, the marking key should be based on some practical experience of using the questions or tasks. These should therefore be pre-tested, which can be done informally in class.

Once it has been written and put into use, a marking key should be discussed in detail and revised as soon as enough experience has been gained. Changes made by common consent among assessors should improve the standard of marking. Such changes may be minor – for example, adding to the lists of particular responses which are considered acceptable, or adjusting the distribution of marks to reward longer responses or discriminate better at a particular level. Clearly, any changes that are made to the test procedure must be reflected by changes in the marking key.

4.5 Mark categories

Not all test systems are intended to test overall proficiency; some aim to assess a specific speaking skill, such as accurate pronunciation, making a formal presentation, or contributing to a debate. Focusing the assessor's attention deliberately on a number of different language skills is also another way to improve marker reliability. The marker is asked to give each learner a separate mark for each category. These separate marks are then combined to give the overall score, either by simple addition or by the process of weighting (see 4.6). This idea is also known as analytic or atomistic marking.

The mark categories are often combined with rating scales for each category to produce a grid or chart. By describing the typical performance in each skill category at each level on the scale, this chart helps the assessor to place each learner correctly.

The kind of categories will probably follow from the teaching programme and will be dictated by the way in which the teaching syllabus expresses the aims of the programme. Crudely speaking, mark categories either follow the traditional model of language components, or they follow the more recent model of performance criteria.

Traditional mark categories concentrate on the language produced, reflecting the view that the accurate command of language is an end in itself, irrespective of who is talking to whom and why. Familiar components of language proficiency commonly used are:

— Grammar
— Vocabulary
— Pronunciation, Intonation and Stress
— Style and Fluency
— Content

Within each of these categories, the assessor might award a mark on the basis of impression ('out of ten marks, I'd give him six for grammar'); or there might be separate score systems for each category. For example, the first three above could be marked subtractively ('subtract one mark for each major error'); style and fluency could be marked on an impression basis and content on an additive system ('score one mark for each of the following points mentioned'). See sections 4.8, 4.9 and 4.10 for further details.

With the shift in emphasis to language as a tool for communication, and not as an end in itself, the more modern style of mark categories requires a consideration of the speaker and the context as well as the correctness of what is said – they cover all aspects of a speaker's 'performance', and are sometimes called 'performance criteria'. For example:

— Size (how long are the utterances produced?)
— Complexity (how far does the speaker attempt complex language?)
— Speed (how fast does he speak?)
— Flexibility (can the speaker adapt quickly to changes in the topic or task?)
— Accuracy (is it correct English?)
— Appropriacy (is the style or register appropriate?)
— Independence (does the speaker rely on a question or stimulus, or can he initiate speech on his own?)
— Repetition (how often does the question or stimulus have to be repeated?)
— Hesitation (how much does the speaker hesitate before and while speaking?)

Some of these criteria, such as size and speed, can be assessed quite objectively, while others, like appropriacy and flexibility, are more difficult to judge. It is not normally feasible for a live assessor to keep track of more than three or four of these criteria at the same time.

Tests that are conducted for special purposes may have corresponding special mark categories. For example, a test for airline cabin staff might have categories for clarity of diction and confidence in manner; a test for teachers might include an assessment of personal enthusiasm or the ability to develop an explanation using supporting evidence.

Some of these categories may seem largely irrelevant to oral proficiency and to be wide open to individual interpretation. As a general rule, the most common categories are the most successful, as they are the most familiar to assessors. Whatever categories you choose must be fully understood by assessors, and preferably be developed by them or at least with their full involvement.

4.6 Weighting

The use of mark categories makes the marking of oral tests easier and more consistent, but if you award the same total of marks for each category you imply that they are all equally important. Many oral test programmes want to reward good performance in some categories more highly than in others, and to do this they use a weighting system.

Weighting is a procedure by which marks are awarded out of the same total for the different mark categories, and these marks are then multiplied by different factors to give them more, or less, influence in the total score. For example, the traditional mark categories described in the previous section might be given the following weighting:

Grammar	marked out of 10 then multiplied by	3
Vocabulary	marked out of 10 then multiplied by	3
Pronunciation	marked out of 10 then multiplied by	2
Fluency, Style	marked out of 10 then multiplied by	1
Content	marked out of 10 then multiplied by	1

This example is clearly weighted in favour of structural accuracy; the mark for grammar is worth three times the mark for content. Rather vague categories such as Fluency or Communication are sometimes included with a low weighting as a token gesture; they do not add much to the overall score or consistency but their presence makes everybody feel better. Markers who are using a strictly analytic system welcome the opportunity to award or not to award extra marks on a more subjective basis: 'He didn't do very well on the structural categories, but I feel that, on the basis of his overall performance, he deserves a couple of extra marks'.

The assumption behind the use of weighting in this way is that it is mentally easier for the assessor to mark all the categories out of the same total initially, and then multiply up the marks to produce a weighted score, than it is to mark one category out of ten, a second out of twenty, and a third out of thirty, at the same time. It is certainly difficult in a live assessment to maintain a strict sense of the relative values of marks out of different totals.

Differential weighting

In a system where the approximate level of each learner is known in advance, and where different tasks are used at the different levels, each category can be given a separate weight for each level. For example, the simple weighting table given above could be adapted, at a higher level, to give more weight to Fluency and Style and less weight to Grammar. This is done in the belief that the contribution made by each category to the overall ability to communicate effectively varies from one level to another.

4.7 Rating scales

A rating scale is a series of short descriptions of different levels of language ability. Its purpose is to describe briefly what the typical learner at each level can do, so that it is easier for the assessor to decide what level or score to give each learner in a test. The rating scale therefore offers the assessor a series of prepared descriptions, and she then picks the one which best fits each learner.

For example, here is a rating scale for general spoken English:

Level 1: Very limited personal conversation.
Knows formulaic greetings and some vocabulary.
Cannot construct correct simple sentences.

Level 2: Personal and limited social conversation.
Can answer simple questions about personal topics correctly in present and past tenses.
Has difficulty with question formation.
Vocabulary still very limited.

Level 3: Basic competence for social and travel uses.
Has basic command of all simple tenses and can operate question and negative forms.
Shows awareness of perfect forms but makes errors in using them.
Familiar with common concrete vocabulary: still searches for words.

Level 4: Elementary professional competence.
Makes effective use of all tenses, including past vs perfect and

simple vs continuous distinctions; occasional errors in tense forms.

Fully active concrete vocabulary and larger passive vocabulary.

Level 5:   General proficiency on all familiar and common topics; may be at a loss for words on other topics, but is able to paraphrase successfully.

Can produce correct complex sentences; very rare errors in structural forms, but makes errors of idiom or collocation.

An immediate problem is that rating scale descriptions can only be built up on the basis of the typical learner, and few learners are typical. Length is a single variable, which can be measured precisely with a ruler; oral language ability is more complex, combining a number of different skills and factors, including personality.

A partial solution is to design a rating scale with several mark categories (see 4.5), one for each of the major language features you think can usefully be isolated. In the table above, each level description in fact contains comments about three language features: general topic of conversation, ability to use tense forms, and vocabulary. This scale could therefore be written with three categories, and if you wished, it would be easy to add a category for pronunciation or listening. Rather than a single description, this gives the assessor a profile of the typical learner at each level, with descriptions of typical performance in four or five areas at that level. However, this leads into another problem.

The second problem is how detailed the profile for each learner should be. The more information you give, the easier it will be for an assessor to find something that seems to match the learner sitting in front of her. At the same time, the more detail at each level, the more likely it is that some of it will be contradictory, or that statements in different categories will seem to place a learner at different levels.

The only solution is to adapt and improve the scales by trial and error, keeping only the parts that are genuinely useful. If you find from experience that a label or description is confusing, try to clarify it; and if you can't do that, drop it. Don't expect to find the perfect scale: if every learner conformed exactly to one of a small number of labels, much of the enjoyment of oral testing would disappear (and so would a lot of teaching jobs!). Where learners come from a homogenous background you can write any consistent features, such as educational experience, into the scale.

Constructing a rating scale

It is important to maintain a continuity between the descriptions at different levels. Particular features may recur at different levels, qualified by labels such as:

> Is not familiar with . . .
> Is aware of . . . but uses incorrectly.
> Has some control of . . . but makes occasional errors.
> Is able to use . . . confidently and accurately.

Qualifiers such as sometimes, most, often, occasionally, are a common feature of the language of rating scales, but it is essential that they relate directly to the learner's performance and not to rating scale descriptions at other levels. If a description says:

Level 6: Makes fewer errors but is only slightly more fluent.

then it only makes sense in relation to other levels, which ultimately leads to a rating scale with circular, self-defining descriptions.

Don't use more levels than you need. If the purpose of the test only requires discrimination of learners into three categories – elementary, intermediate and advanced – then designing a rating scale with more than three levels is unnecessary hard work. The fewer levels you have, the easier it is to assess, and the higher the reliability will be. Keep it as simple as possible. A rating scale will only work well if the assessor can hold it in her mind while listening or talking to the learner, and does not have to keep referring to a large manual to tell her what to look for.

It may be helpful to look for a range, not a point on a scale. A learner's performance usually varies during an oral test, showing strong and weak points, or perhaps a nervous start and a more confident finish. If the range is very wide, find the highest level at which the learner can sustain his performance more or less consistently. Occasional flashes of brilliance which are not sustained should be ignored, as should a single serious error; only consistent patterns of strength and weakness should be compared against the rating scale to produce an assessment.

4.8 Impression marking

The assessor awards a mark based on the learner's overall performance, without picking out any special features or using a counting system for errors. This assessment may be made with reference to a rating scale (see 4.7). It can be done on a single scale for the whole test or done for certain individual mark categories (see 4.5). Single-scale impression marking is often used as a rough-and-ready guide for quick placement or progress tests where there is little time for complicated marking systems, and errors of judgement can always be corrected afterwards.

Where different mark categories are used, they will often be marked by different systems: this is not a sign of inconsistency, but rather reflects the fact that they are measuring very different things. Impression marking is used for the kind of categories that are very hard to define but everybody agrees are important: fluency, ability to communicate, style, naturalness of speech, and so on. (In a major essay-marking experiment in the 1940s, the inclusion of an extra impression-based mark category of this kind was found not to improve the reliability of the mark system, but it was recommended because all the markers themselves said they liked it!)

Impression-based marking calls for subjective judgement in its most positive sense. Whenever we talk to a foreigner in our native language we make a judgement about his language ability. It may not even be conscious, but we automatically form a subjective, personal opinion of the foreigner's communicative ability in the real world. It is the sum of all these personal judgements made by all the people the foreigner speaks to that finally determines how well he has communicated: deliberate and careful impression-based marking is the most direct and authentic reflection of this real-life process that it is possible to have in an oral test.

As in the real world we might be reluctant to rely on a single impression judgement by one person, so in oral testing we try to design a testing/ marking system that provides other evidence to support an impression mark. Making accurate impression-based assessments requires a lot of experience, and less experienced assessors would not normally be expected to make assessments based on impression alone. Even experienced assessors find it difficult to make consistent impression-based judgements. If it is not possible to have a second live assessor, or a rater checking from a tape, then an impression mark can be combined with a score from another test or marking system.

4.9   Additive marking

The assessor has a prepared list of features to listen out for during the test. She awards a mark for each of these features that the learner produces correctly, and adds these marks to give the score. This is also known as an incremental mark system; the learner starts with a score of zero and earns each mark, one by one.

The term 'feature' used in this description is deliberately vague. Additive marks can be awarded for:

— Content features, such as the mention of particular events, actions or attributes that are important to a story or description; the use of social formulae in situations where they can be considered obligatory; the use of introductory, summarising and closing remarks in a formal presentation; and so on.
— Grammatical structures or sentence patterns; these can either be fixed

in advance and deliberately elicited, or the assessor can note the grammatical patterns used and score according to a pre-determined system.
— Specific vocabulary items.
— Pronunciation, stress or intonation features in reading particular passages aloud.
— The number of sentences correctly produced; the overall score is derived by subtracting the number of incorrect ones.

The additive mark system is used for test techniques or mark categories where it is possible to prepare a list of such features to listen for. It is simple to operate and very reliable; the assessor has only to decide whether certain pre-selected features were correctly produced or not. But in order to make this possible, the techniques used must be restricted in such a way that all the learners are going to say virtually the same thing, in order to make their scores truly comparable.

4.10 Subtractive marking

The assessor subtracts one mark from a total for each mistake the learner makes, down to a minimum of zero. There may be a single subtractive category for all errors, with some general name such as 'mechanics', 'structure' or 'form', or there may be separate subtractive categories for features such as 'grammar', 'vocabulary' and 'pronunciation'. Normally one mark is deducted for each definite error from a starting total of, for example, ten, but sometimes a distinction is made between a major error (1 mark off) and a minor error (½ mark off). This seems a more just system for the learner but it makes the assessor's job harder as she has to decide in each case whether an error was a major or minor one, when no such convenient distinction exists in reality.

The subtractive mark system is quite easy to apply. It requires continuous assessor training to ensure that everybody agrees about what is an error and what is not. When that agreement is reached, it is a reliable marking technique. Although a marking key to aid the assessor can easily be produced (listing the most common errors), it is impossible to predict every error; it will therefore be necessary to formulate simple rules describing how error gravity is to be judged, and this is not an easy task.

Subtractive marking is commonly used for categories such as 'structure' and 'vocabulary', but is unsuitable for more general categories like 'content' or 'style', where mistakes are almost impossible to agree on consistently. Although a learner who makes many mistakes is unlikely on the whole to communicate well, a mark system that relies entirely on subtractive marking will penalise the effective, but inaccurate, communicator. This system of scoring by penalty is a negative one, and leads the assessor to concentrate on searching for mistakes at the expense of the positive points about the learner's speech. If the aim of the test is to assess accuracy of speech, subtractive marking alone will be sufficient, but for a balanced assessment of overall spoken proficiency, it is desirable to combine it with other marking techniques.

5 Test evaluation

The purpose of this book has been to encourage teachers and testers to experiment with oral testing ideas, rather than automatically follow a test procedure taken from somewhere else. In any kind of experiment you watch closely to see what the results are; if it doesn't work well, you change the design and try it again. This requires an effective system for evaluation.

Test evaluation answers the question, 'Does the test work properly?' Because the phrase 'work properly' can be interpreted in different ways, the question has different kinds of answer. The general term for how well a test works is 'validity', and this too has a variety of meanings. This chapter looks at the different kinds of validity, and how they can be assessed.

It is important to realise that this ambiguity is a central feature of validity, not just an irritation that sometimes gets in the way. Because you have to ask different kinds of questions about validity, you get different kinds of answers, and these answers will often conflict. Before you can make any decisions about improving the test you have to strike a balance between these conflicting answers. This tension is fundamental to test evaluation; there is never a single answer to the question, 'Does the test work properly?' The best test is the one that strikes the right balance for your particular programme.

The process of establishing the general validity of a test procedure is called validation. It depends on the situation in which the test is used as much as the test itself. Validation is a relative, and not an absolute, process; the degree of validity of a test relates only to the particular circumstances in which it was established. You cannot determine that a test has a certain validity in one testing programme, and expect it to have the same validity when applied to a completely different situation.

Types of validity

There are two ways to approach the general question, 'Does the test work properly?' One way is to ask people what they think of the contents and design of the test; particularly the people who use it, such as the learners, the teachers, the administrators and the people who take decisions based on the results. None of them may be experts in testing, but their opinions are important because they have to live with the test every day. Expert opinion is highly desirable if it is available; but if nobody who is directly involved likes the test, then it is not a very good test, even if it seems excellent in other ways. We can call these *personal* judgements of validity (see 5.1, 5.2 and 5.3).

The other type of question asks for numerical answers: are the test results consistent? How does a new test compare with other recognised tests? These are questions about the *statistical* measures of validity (see 5.4, 5.5 and 5.6).

For the purpose of this discussion, I have included reliability as a specific form of validity. Reliability is usually seen as a completely different concept from validity, and the two terms are presented in terms of mutual incompatibility: highly reliable tests are less valid, and vice versa. Particularly in oral testing, I prefer to see reliability as a specific type of general validity; a test cannot be generally valid (in the sense 'Does the test work?') unless it is reliable.

Both reliability and validity are rather vague concepts which suffer from a lack of clear definition about exactly what they are, let alone how they should be assessed or calculated. From a practical point of view, the important point is to answer the question, 'Does the test do what it's supposed to?', and reliability, like other specific forms of validity, provides one kind of answer to this question.

All aspects of validity are important, and as much information as possible about the different types of validity (described below) should be collected. When that information has been collected, then it must be carefully and critically sifted, always bearing in mind the aims of the programme, and a balanced answer to the question, 'Does the test work properly?' can be given. Unfortunately, there has been a tendency among so-called language testing experts to base test evaluation too much on statistical measures; this makes it seem terribly scientific and objective, but it also endangers the intuitive judgement of normally sensible men and women. Common sense is the tester's best friend.

An oral test is a personal encounter between two human beings; it is designed by humans, administered by humans, taken by humans and marked by humans, and it would be a surrender of the test designer's responsibility to allow the evaluation and development of this wholly human activity to be dictated by the statistical sausage-machine.

5.1   Face validity

On the face of it, does it look like a reasonable test? Do the people who use the test think it's a good test? If either the testers or the learners are unhappy with it, then it won't yield good results. Clearly, the best way of researching this form of validity is to question the different people who come into contact with the test. Learners generally produce very informative and objective comments about tests, irrespective of their own personal performance; any doubts about this can be easily checked by comparing the general tone of their comments with their scores.

5.2 Content validity

Is it relevant? Do the items or tasks in the test match what the test as a whole is supposed to assess? In other words, does the test match the aims and needs that were set out in chapter 1? Where the objectives of the programme are set out in detail, for example in a syllabus that lists skills or functions, then the content validity can be assessed by comparing the kind of language generated in the test against the syllabus. The question then is whether the test produces a good sample of the contents of the syllabus.

Where the aims of the programme are set out in more general terms – or, frequently, not set out at all – content validity is harder to establish because there is nothing specific to compare the language of the test with. Validation must then rely to a great extent on the test designer's intuitive knowledge of the implicit objectives of the programme.

5.3 Construct validity

Does the test match the theory behind it? Almost all tests are part of a larger programme; and every programme makes some basic assumptions, explicitly or implicitly, about the purposes and processes of language learning. A test should obviously share the same assumptions and the same philosophy as the programme of which it is part. For example, if the teaching programme aims to give learners a limited competence in particular professional areas, using a lot of exposure to authentic language and documents, then the test procedure should follow the same basic approach.

A lot of the work that has been done recently with factor analysis (see the Introduction) has attempted to establish construct validity by statistical rather than intuitive means. The statistically naive reader – and for that matter, the expert too – should be extremely cautious of interpreting the results of such statistical analyses as solid evidence for any particular theoretical construct.

Construct validity is not an easy idea to work with, and indeed may not have much value outside language testing research. To reduce it to its simplest statement it says: does the test match your views on language learning? In practice, there may be little difference between construct and content validity.

5.4 Reliability

Are markers consistent with themselves in the scores they give, or do their standards vary from day to day? Are there big differences in the marks awarded by different markers? Does the test procedure itself seem to produce consistent scores?

Two different statistical procedures are commonly used to produce estimates of reliability. These are correlation and Kuder–Richardson internal consistency formulae. They can be carried out using a pocket calculator; the problem, as always, is one of interpretation rather than calculation. The two Kuder–Richardson formulae used, and each of the three common procedures based on correlation – test/re-test, parallel form and split-half – all make different assumptions about what is being tested, how constant it is over time, the possibility of devising two different but exactly equivalent tests, and so on.

These classical measures of test reliability have little relevance for oral tests because they are designed for rigid, pre-planned tests consisting of a fixed number of individual questions, each of which the learner gets individually right or wrong. They concentrate on the test itself, as an independent object. But most oral tests are not like lists of questions on paper; they do not exist separately from the people who take part in them.

The test designer will get more useful information by designing her own system for comparing each marker's scores with her own scores at a later date, and with the scores of other markers. This will tell her which markers are the most consistent with themselves; which markers consistently over-rate or under-rate compared to others; which marking systems produce the most reliable results between markers, and which techniques are the hardest to mark consistently.

Once the testing and marking systems have been chosen, some careful reflection and discussion, and a lot of common sense, will suggest a simple way to produce the particular information about reliability that is most important to that programme. Sophisticated statistical knowledge should certainly be used if it is available, but the most useful and easily-interpreted information will only require the ability to add, subtract and calculate averages.

5.5 Concurrent validity

How do learners' scores on the test compare with their scores on other language tests? The same learners' scores on a new test procedure are correlated with their scores on an established test which has already been independently validated; this produces a correlation coefficient which suggests the extent to which the tests are measuring the same thing. This is concurrent validity. One would logically expect two different oral test scores to correlate more highly than one oral test score with a multiple-choice grammar test score.

What you logically expect, however, doesn't always happen, and as always with statistics it is the interpretation that is the hardest part. A high correlation – 0.9 or more – strongly suggests that the tests are measuring the same thing, and a low correlation – 0.4 or less – suggests that they are measuring substantially different things. The vast majority of correlation coefficients fall somewhere in between these figures, and no single conclusion can be drawn from them. The size and variety of the sample, the type of task or question used, the reliability of the tests, and the attitudes of the learners, testers and markers can all affect the significance of a correlation.

5.6 Predictive validity

Can the test predict how successful the learners will be at using the language in the future? The learners' scores on the new test are correlated against their performance on some important task at some future point. For example, if you were training switchboard operators to do their job in a foreign language, you would correlate their scores on your test against as realistic a measure as possible of how well they can operate in the foreign language when they get back to work.

If you have clear objectives for your test, it would be highly desirable to be able to establish a degree of predictive validity for the test against those objectives. Unfortunately, predictive validity correlations are even harder to interpret with confidence than concurrent validity correlations. This is because of all the different influences that can affect the learners' abilities and performance between the two test measures. The longer the interval of time between the two test measures being correlated, the less trust can be placed in the result.

Appendix I Three public oral tests

The purpose of this appendix is to give some practical examples of how the techniques mentioned in this book are used in practice. It describes three oral test procedures that are commercially available on their own or as part of larger proficiency test batteries. In each case, the oral test consists of a sequence of at least three of the test techniques described in the previous chapters. Most of the descriptions below are taken directly or paraphrased from the handbooks or instructions issued by the examining authority, details of which are given in Appendix II.

1 University of Cambridge Local Examinations Syndicate (UCLES)

First Certificate and Certificate of Proficiency in English

These examinations include an oral interview as one of five subtests. It lasts twelve to fifteen minutes, and may be conducted either between a single candidate and the examiner, or between a group of candidates with an interlocutor.

The interview consists of a theme-based conversation, based on a package of materials designed to elicit discussion and comment on the theme using a variety of different techniques and stimuli including pictures, short passages and realia. Examples of themes used in practice materials are 'Weather' and 'Adventure/ Taking Risks'.

The examiner's material consists of a number of packages of theme-based sets of photographs and other prompts from which the complete interview is conducted. The photograph has sets of suggested questions and follow-up topics. The conversation should move from specific commentary on the situation shown in the picture to associated themes, with the candidates encouraged to speak freely.

A passage is then selected and the candidate is given a few moments to look through it before being encouraged to identify its probable source and intention and relate it as appropriate to the general theme of the discussion. Full reading aloud of the passage is not required, but candidates may quote from it where this is appropriate to the discussion.

The interview is completed either by a discussion of a piece of authentic material and/or a communicative activity using a variety of visual and verbal stimuli. The range of activities includes participation in a role-playing exercise, finding out information, giving and exchanging opinions, and problem-solving discussion. There is often an 'information-gap' between the participants.

The marking system is based on six mark categories for the whole test: Fluency, Grammatical Accuracy, Pronunciation (sentences and individual sounds), Interactive Communication and Vocabulary Resource. The examiner makes an impression-based judgement for each mark category, using outline rating scales provided.

2   Association of Recognised English Language Schools Examination Trust

The AET administers oral examinations at three levels – Preliminary, Higher, and Diploma – which are conducted entirely in a language laboratory. Candidates anywhere in the world listen to an identical master tape, and their responses are recorded on personal tapes, which are then sent in for marking. This ensures a complete standardisation of the giving of instructions and stimuli, of the vocabulary and intonation used, and the time allotted for the candidate's response. The total length of the test is 35–50 minutes, depending on level.

This uniformity of test administration allows a detailed marking key to be used for the marking of every tape. At the two higher levels all the tapes are double-marked, and at the Preliminary level ten per cent are double-marked, including borderline cases.

The Preliminary level has three main sections, and the Higher and Diploma levels, six sections. Each section may contain more than one sub-section. As well as activities that specifically test aural comprehension, the following speaking tasks may be included:

– making appropriate responses
– reading aloud, text or part of dialogue
– answering comprehension questions on recorded text or dialogue
– narrating story from picture cues
– describing a picture
– summarising recorded passage (with own opinion welcomed)
– sentence transformation and question formation
– giving short talk on chosen topic
– interpreting stress and intonation patterns

The selection and order of techniques used varies from one examination to another. There is often no clear division between one activity and the next, as two or more activities may relate to the same theme.

3   Royal Society of Arts (RSA) Examinations in the Communicative Use of English as a Foreign Language

Oral Interaction is one of the four tests in this new examination, and it can be taken together either with, or independently of, the tests in the other three skills. Each test is offered at three levels: Basic, Intermediate and Advanced. The oral test has three parts, each lasting about five minutes, which differ mainly in terms of who is speaking to whom.

1. The candidate talks to an interlocutor, in the presence of an assessor, about a pre-set task, about himself, or about his language background.
2. Two candidates discuss together, in the presence of the assessor only, a subject of some topical interest. Other than ensuring that the candidates understand the task, the assessor takes no direct part. When the task is completed ...
3. The interlocutor comes in, and the candidates have to tell her what it is they have been saying and what decisions they have come to.

Parts 2 and 3 thus share a common theme; in part 3 the candidates report and comment on what happened in part 2. The tasks set generally require some kind of choice to be made or decision to be reached, and the instructions tell the candidates that they should be prepared to give reasons for the choice or justify the decision. It is important that this should be done otherwise part 3 is merely a recapitulation of part 2.

The interlocutor's role is to help the candidates perform as well as they can. She should as far as possible respond to what the candidates say in such a way as to encourage further interaction or explanation, rather than directing the conversation or interviewing the candidates.

The marking of the oral interaction is done by comparison of the candidate's performance against the degree of skill required for each level in the RSA specifications. For parts 2 and 3, different tasks are used at each level to reflect the wider range of operations expected of candidates at higher levels. Although she is still making a personal judgement, the assessor's task is made easier in that she has essentially to make a Yes/No decision – does each person's performance meet the criteria set out in the specifications, or not?

Appendix II: Bibliography and further reading

Introduction

For a fascinating read on the history of mental testing, and the nonsensical use of statistics, see chapters 5 and 6 of:
Stephen Jay Gould, *The Mismeasure of Man* (New York, Norton, 1981)

The quotation on page 4 'sophisticated statistics poised on testing techniques of rustic simplicity' comes from:
Liam Hudson, *Contrary Imaginations* (Penguin, 1967), p. 13
This is a highly readable and entertaining book, which should serve as an example of how mental testing can be carried out in a human way, to yield common-sense results. In the introductory chapter, Presuppositions, he describes how, after an initial period of rapid innovation, the actual tests themselves stagnated; instead, all the energy of the pioneers in the field went into the development of ever more complex statistics.

> 'One wonders why progress should have been so slow; and it seems that a quality of isolation, or *incapsulation*, is the crucial one. In a variety of ways, mental testers have sealed themselves off from the human subject-matter which would have ensured them, if not per-petual youth and perplexity, at least a livelier middle age. And in this process of incapsulation, statistics have played an insidious part . . . Indeed, it has been suggested that the contribution of mental testing has been primarily to the theory of statistics itself, rather than to psychology or education.' (pp. 13–14)

He is writing about mental testers, but the comments about isolation from the human subject matter fit language testers exactly. It should remind us that mainstream language testing, and language testing research in particular, owes more to psychometry than it does to language learning and teaching.

Chapter 1

More about needs analysis in:
J. L. Munby, *Communicative Syllabus Design* (Cambridge University Press, 1978)
Brendan J. Carroll, *Testing Communicative Performance* (Pergamon, 1980)
Both of these suffer from an excessive use of jargon.

Chapter 2

2.1   For a lot more excellent detail on self-assessment, see:
Mats Oskarsson, *Approaches to Self-Assessment in Foreign Language Learning*, Council of Europe (Pergamon, 1980)

2.3   The quotation, 'there were no victims, only active agents' comes from:
Linda Lombardo, 'Oral testing: getting a sample of the real language', in *English Teaching Forum*, 22/1 (1984)
To put it in context:

> 'Although the teacher–examiner was free to call on a student for a summary, to decide how far to pursue it, or even to probe a particular point at the end of the student exchange, the students knew that the main part of the test was in their hands, and it was perhaps this sense of control that gave them greater confidence and allowed them to show off their English. In other words, there were no victims, only active agents.' (p. 4)

Chapter 3

3.1   The terms *control* and *initiative* are used in Stevick's sense, for example in:
Earl W. Stevick, *Teaching Languages: a Way and Ways* (Newbury House, 1980)
Control consists of providing a framework or structure for what happens, like setting the rules of a game; *initiative* means the individual decisions about who says what and when, like individual moves in the game, subject to the general rules.

3.3   For some excellent ideas for group discussion topics and tasks, see:
Friederike Klippel, *Keep Talking* (Cambridge University Press, 1984)
   For an example of how variation 1 is used, see:
David Golland and David Robertson, 'Towards objectivity in group oral testing', *ELT Journal*, 30/2 (1976)

3.4   For a successful example of variation 1, the learner–learner role-play, see:
Linda Lombardo, 'Oral testing: getting a sample of the real language', in *English Teaching Forum*, 22/1 (1984)

3.5   The most thorough and detailed treatment of the oral interview is:
ETS Oral Proficiency Testing Manual (Educational Testing Service, Princeton, New Jersey, 1982)

3.8   For some examples and variations of the Appropriate Response technique, see:
Jan van Weeren, 'Testing oral proficiency in everyday situations' in C. Klein Braley and D. K. Stevenson (eds.), *Practice and Problems in Language Testing*, vol. 1 (Frankfurt/Bern, 1981)

3.11   For an example of the similar but different pictures used for variation 1, see:
William Littlewood, *Communicative Language Teaching* (Cambridge University Press, 1981)
    For some more variations on this theme, see:
A. S. Palmer, 'Testing communication' in *IRAL*, 10/1 (1972)
    For extensive use of the little clock faces in variation 5, see:
Donna Ilyin, *The Ilyin Interview Test* (Newbury House, 1976)

3.15   The idea for variation 3 came from:
Jonquil Hole, 'Pronunciation testing – what did you say?', *ELT Journal*, 37/2 (1983)

Chapter 4

4.8   The essay marking experiment is described in detail in:
P. Hartog et al., *The Marking of English Essays* (Macmillan, London, 1941)
The extra mark category was called, very simply, 'sense'. Although their work was solely concerned with marking written work, they tackled many of the same problems that face oral test designers.

Chapter 5

5.1, 5.3   For the most patronising example of expert disregard for face validity, and of the attempt to annex construct – i.e. theoretical – validity into the empire of statistics, see:
Douglas K. Stevenson, 'Beyond faith and face validity: the multitrait-multimethod matrix and the convergent and discriminant validity of oral proficiency tests' in Adrian S. Palmer, Peter J. M. Groot and George A. Trosper (eds.), *The Construct Validation of Tests of Communicative Competence* (Washington DC, TESOL, 1981)

5.4   For a good practical discussion of reliability, see:
R. L. Thorndike and E. P. Hagen, *Measurement and Evaluation in Psychology and Education*, 4th edn (New York, John Wiley, 1977)

5.4–5.6   A straightforward reference book for correlations and many other elementary statistical procedures is:
Ray Meddis, *Statistical Handbook for Non-Statisticians* (London, McGraw-Hill, 1975)

Appendix 1

The quotations and descriptions are based on:
UCLES:
– The Teacher's Book for CPE Practice Tests 2 (CUP 1987).
– Instructions to Oral Examiners 1985.
UCLES is at Syndicate Buildings, 1 Hills Road, Cambridge CB1 2EU, UK.

ARELS:
– ARELS Oral Examinations in Spoken English: Rationale, Development and Methods.
– The Oxford–ARELS Examinations in English as a Foreign Language: Regulations and Syllabuses.
The ARELS Examination Trust is at 113 Banbury Road, Oxford OX2 6JX, UK.

RSA:
– The Communicative Use of English as a Foreign Language.
The RSA is at John Adam Street, Adelphi, London WC2N 6EZ, UK.

Index